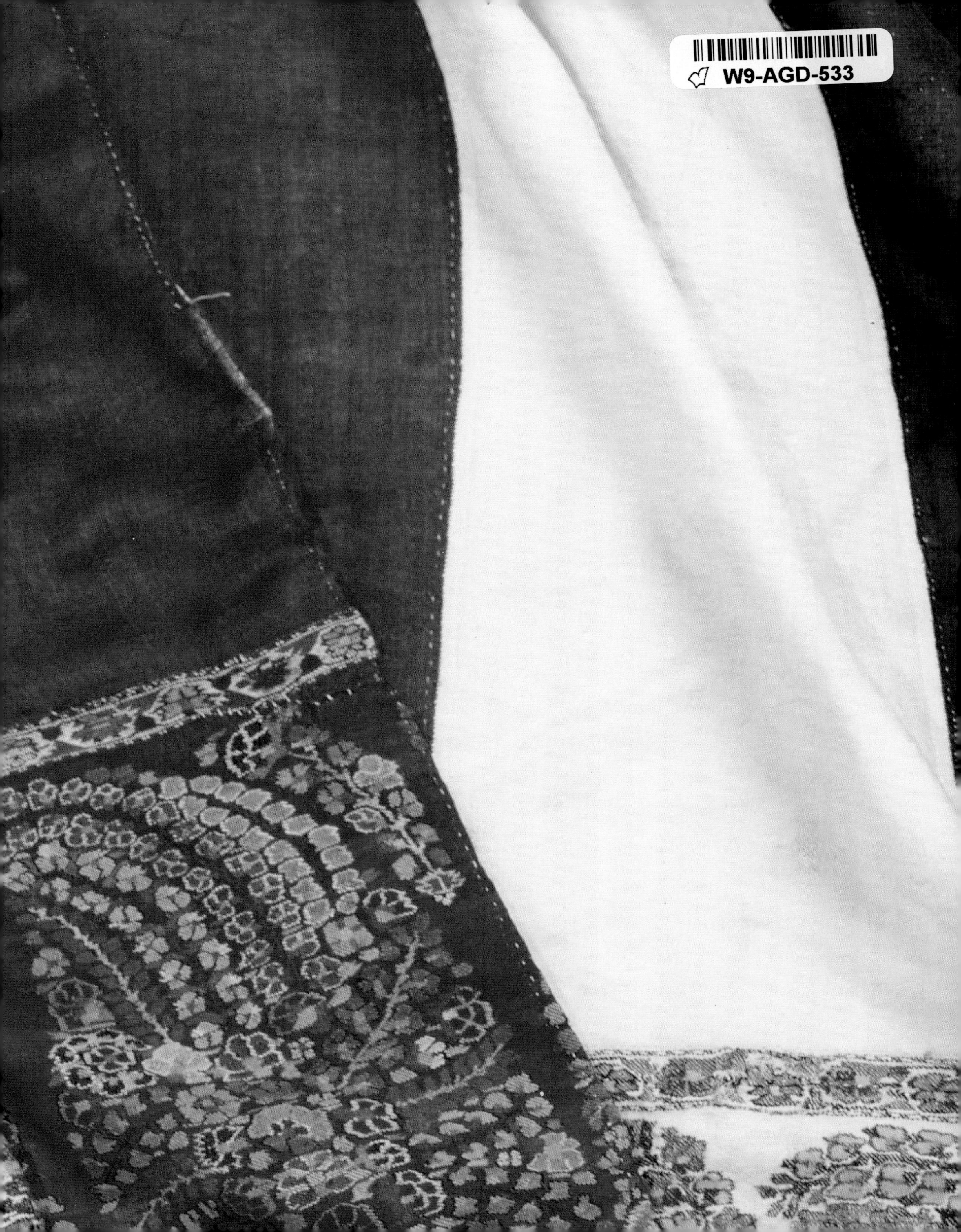

NAPOLEON

NAPOLEON

THE STEWART
MUSEUM
AT THE FORT
ÎLE SAINTE-HÉLÈNE

Catalogue of the exhibition *Napoleon ... at Île Sainte-Hélène*,
presented by the Stewart Museum at the Fort, Île Sainte-Hélène from May 5 to October 11, 1999

Exhibition Committee
Bernard Chevallier, Director
Musée national des châteaux de Malmaison et Bois-Préau

Guy Vadeboncoeur, Chief Curator,
The Stewart Museum at the Fort, Île Sainte-Hélène

Editor
Sylvie Dauphin

Revision of French texts
Mireille Hardy

Translation and English revision
Jill Corner

Revision
Eileen Meillon

Photographic documentation
Angeline Dazé, Nadia Hammadi, Éric Pautrel, Giles Rivest

Graphic design
Charpentier Garneau Communications

This exhibition has received financial support from the City of Montréal, the Ministry of Foreign Affairs and International Trade of Canada (Youth International Internship Program) and Power Corporation of Canada.

© David M. Stewart Museum
ISBN 0–921351–05–4 (French edition)
ISBN 0–921351–06–2 (English edition)
Legal deposit: 2nd quarter 1999
Bibliothèque nationale du Québec
National Library of Canada

Stewart Museum at the Fort, Île Sainte-Hélène
P.O. Box 1200, Station A,
Montreal, Quebec, Canada H3C 2Y9
www.stewart-museum.org

Printed in Canada

NAPOLEON

Published under the direction of
Bernard Chevallier
Director of the Musée national des châteaux de Malmaison et Bois-Préau

Texts by
Bernard Chevallier,
Guy Vadeboncoeur,
Robert Derome
and **Jean-François Gauvin**

The Stewart Museum at the Fort, Île Sainte-Hélène
Montreal, Quebec

List of Lenders

Our gratitude is hereby expressed to all those who helped in the preparation of this exhibition.

Private collections

Élaine Bédard - Alexandre de Bothuri Báthory, Palm Beach, United States of America

Malmaison Antiques, New York, United States of America

The Honourable Serge Joyal, Senator, P.C., O.C., Montreal, Canada

Éric Pautrel, Rueil-Malmaison, France

Power Corporation of Canada, Montreal, Canada

Roger Prigent, New York, United States of America

Ben Weider, Montreal, Canada

Public Collections

Archives de Paris, Paris, France

The Bata Shoe Museum, Toronto, Canada

Bibliothèque Marmottan, Boulogne Billancourt, France

Bibliothèque nationale du Québec, Montreal, Canada

Château-Musée de l'Empéri, Salon-de-Provence, France

Ministère de la Défense, Service historique de l'Armée de Terre, Vincennes, France

Ministère des Affaires Étrangères, Direction des archives, Paris, France

Mobilier National, Paris, France

Musée de l'Armée, Paris, France

Musée du Château Ramezay, Montreal, Canada

Musée Marmottan-Claude Monet, Paris, France

Musée national de la Céramique, Sèvres, France

Musée national de la coopération franco-américaine, Blérancourt, France

Musée national de la Légion d'honneur et des ordres de chevalerie, Paris, France

Musée national de la Maison Bonaparte, Ajaccio, France

Musée national de l'île d'Aix, Fondation Gourgaud, île d'Aix, France

Musée national des châteaux de Malmaison et Bois-Préau, Rueil-Malmaison, France

Musée national du château de Fontainebleau, Fontainebleau, France

Musée national du château de Versailles, Versailles, France

ACKNOWLEDGEMENTS

We wish to express our gratitude for their invaluable help to
the following persons and institutions:

Cory McAdam, Beaconsfield, Quebec
Diane Bernier Design, Sainte-Thérèse, Quebec
Anne Desjardins, Montreal, Quebec
Dionne et LeBlanc Communications, Montreal, Québec
Bruno Donzet, Prospective et Patrimoine, Paris, France
Guy Ducharme, Macdonald Stewart Foundation, Montreal, Quebec
Nicole Lemay, Town of Mount Royal, Quebec
Andrew Mahon, Montreal, Quebec
Albert Millaire, Montreal, Quebec
Navicom, Montreal, Quebec
Éric Pautrel, Musée national des châteaux de Malmaison et de Bois-Préau, France
Ramsay International, Montreal, Quebec

Bruce D. Bolton, Director
And the staff of the Stewart Museum

Thierry Bois d'Enghien, Henriette Barbeau, Éric Brouillard, Philip Butler,
Louis-Philippe Carrier, Sylvia Deschênes, Louise Duchesneau, Robert Galteri,
Céline Gignac, Lise Giguère, Nelson Heppell, Zély Jean, François Lambert,
Françoise Lambert, Éric Michaud and the team of guide-animators,
Jean-Claude Papineau, Nicolas Paradis and Normand Trudel

Dimensions are expressed in centimeter in the following order:
Height, Length, Width.

Contents

For two centuries now, much has been said and reams written about Napoleon Bonaparte. The brilliant achievements of this almost legendary figure have inspired artists and intrigued whole generations. As a new millennium dawns, the cult of Napoleon is still very much alive, as can be seen in the exhibitions, among other manifestations, that have been devoted to the subject by museums across the world in the last ten years.

Our Museum has always taken a special interest in the Emperor and in the other characters involved in the many achievements of his reign. In 1964 we presented a small exhibition entitled "Napoleon and the Canadians" which retraced the story of the pioneers' sons who went to win glory under the Empire. We are consequently very happy today to present a major exhibition on Napoleon Bonaparte, *Napoleon … at Île Sainte-Hélène* to enable our public to discover this rich cultural and artistic heritage through documents, images and priceless objects from collections abroad brought to Montreal and to Canada for the first time.

This exhibition would not have been possible without the invaluable support of M. Bernard Chevallier, director of the Musée national des châteaux de Malmaison et de Bois-Préau. From the very start his unshakeable confidence in the venture never wavered. M. Chevallier placed his talent, efficacy and experience entirely at the service of the exhibition. The catalogue of the show, of which he is the main author, reflects not only his immense knowledge of the subject but also his unflagging enthusiasm and commitment to our project. I would like to express here my deep gratitude for his outstanding contribution.

I must also thank for their kind cooperation the many museums, libraries, archival institutions and private collectors who have so generously loaned us rare and often unique pieces.

I invite you to share our fascination with these objects and works of art so closely linked to the extraordinary Napoleonic adventure and to one of the great figures of world history.

Mrs. David M. Stewart
Chair
The Stewart Museum

As fate would have it, Napoleon was born in Ajaccio on August 15, 1769, just as the troops of King Louis XV of France were taking possession of Corsica. The future Emperor's father, Charles BONAPARTE, was an influential lawyer in Ajaccio. In 1764 he married Letizia Ramolino, a girl of fourteen; there followed thirteen pregnancies before Charles died in 1785. He had used his French citizenship to obtain recognition of the Bonaparte family as noble and, taking advantage of the privileges of rank, enrolled young NAPOLEON first in the Military College at Brienne and then in the Royal Military College, Paris.

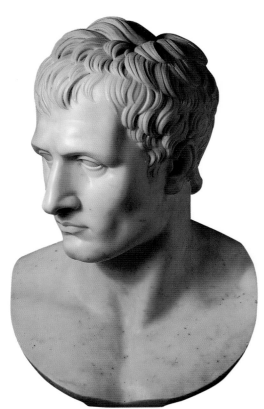

4

Workshops of Carrara, after Antonio Canova
(1757–1822)

Monumental bust of Napoleon as First Consul

New York, Roger Prigent collection
Marble
H. 66; L. 48.3
About 1810

Commencing from a bust modelled at Saint-Cloud in five sittings during the fall of 1802, Canova executed a monumental statue of Napoleon as Mars the Pacifier weighing thirteen tons. It was transported to Paris, not without difficulty, in 1811 but being a portrayal in the nude it displeased the Emperor and was kept from public view throughout the Empire. In 1816 it was purchased by the British government and presented to Wellington, who had it installed in the stairwell of Aspley House, his London residence. The great beauty of the head so impressed Élisa, Grand Duchess of Tuscany, that she had the work reproduced in her workshop at Carrara by the sculptor Lorenzo Bartolini. Though it cost 2000 francs on arrival in Paris, the retail price was only 448.60 francs, which left Élisa a substantial profit. A number of high-quality copies are still extant, most of them commissioned by municipalities wishing to honour the Emperor.

What can we say that has not already been said about Napoleon? The subject is inexhaustible. It is usual to remark that more books on him have been published than days have elapsed since his death. And nothing can stop the passage of time. How not to repeat what others have said, how to avoid boring the public, how to approach the question in an original manner without resorting to clichés: this was the challenge willingly faced by the authors of the catalogue accompanying the Montreal international exhibition "Napoleon ... at Île Sainte-Hélène".

Napoleon said: *"500 years from now, the French will dream only of me."* Two centuries later they are not alone in this. Napoleon's popularity has not stopped growing since he himself decided to promote it. The man left no one indifferent: people loved him or hated him. He kept constant control over information, allowing nothing to be made public that did not glorify his regime and, of course, himself. *"What is government? Nothing without public opinion"* he wrote to the Duke of Lodi in 1803. He was very aware of the importance of public opinion and kept an eye on all that was said, done and written, as is evident from the great output of works of art celebrating his audacity, his achievements and his moments of glory, even in defeat.

The Emperor always made the right gesture, turned up in the right place and used the right word; his retorts were cutting, his arguments sound and unshakeable. In reading his words, whether authentic or attributed to him, we discover a remarkable strength of character. He was close to his soldiers and gave them heart. Bulletins from the Grand Army publicised throughout France his brillant successes, great deeds and victories. Napoleon had an almost magnetic power over men. His phenomenal memory, his gift for mathematics, his physical and nervous energy, his powers of recuperation, his ability to concentrate, analyse, order and solve problems, his nerve and personal courage, made a deep impression on everyone who who knew him or met him, even if only once.

And so a legend was born.

1

Boc containing various mementoes from St. Helena of Napoleon and his family, collected by Marchand, the Emperor's valet

Musée national des châteaux de Malmaison et Bois-Préau;
MM 40–47–3090/3098
Carved wood, dead leaves, glass, metal
Gift of Comte Raoul Desmazières-Marchand
H. 46; L. 31
Mid-19th century

2
Delaunay

Poster showing Napoleon on horseback

Musée national des châteaux de Malmaison et Bois-Préau; MM 58-3-538
Gift of Princess George of Greece (formerly the Demidoff Collection, Prince of San Donato, later Prince Roland Bonaparte, the donor's father)
Paper, colour
H. 77; L. 52
1894

It is not surprising, then, that from the beginning of the Empire, indeed, from the Italian campaign on, Bonaparte was recognised as extraordinary. Objects recording his deeds and words began to be manufactured. These modest testimonies to the cult of the Emperor, often handmade, began to circulate in Napoleon's lifetime, and the phenomenon persists. From snuffboxes to rings, pipes to paperknives, all these items spread abroad the image of the great man and the incredible stories told of him.

In 1958 several thousand such objects were given to the Musée de Malmaison by the widow of Prince George of Greece and Denmark (1869-1957), a passionate collector of such things. Née Marie Bonaparte (1882-1962), a psychoanalyst and student of Freud, she was the great-granddaughter of Lucien, the Emperor's brother. Stamps with Napoleon's head crossed cities, seas and continents, while collections of Napoleonic memorabilia were found worldwide, from figurines to objects of value.

And so the legend went on.

Modern advertisers, without even referring to Napoleonic legend, have used the "image"
of Napoleon as a trademark, a symbol of prestige, of mathematical strategy
and guaranteed victory, an image that sells more products. We still see this
trademark today.

The twentieth century, the communications age, has not escaped the Napoleonic legend.
Over 120 films about Napoleon and his times have been made since 1897: on film,
in plays, operas and musical comedies (one of the most recent by Serge Lama), at
least as many actors have played Napoleon, tried to get inside his head, feel as he
did and convey that emotion to the audience.

And so the legend goes on down the centuries...

G.V.

3

Jean-Pierre-Marie Jazet
(1788–1871),
after Horace Vernet
(1789–1863)

Napoleon Coming out of the Tomb

Musée national des châteaux
de Malmaison et Bois-préau
(Fonds Napoléon);
N 2569; Purchase, 1979 (formerly the
collections of the Imperial family)
Colour print on paper
H. 61,5; L. 48,2
1840

Like another Christ, the Emperor comes
forth from his tomb, pushing back the
shadows around him; the idol of a secu-
lar religion in which he is regarded as a
messiah, Napoleon became a rallying
symbol for various movements united in
the same struggle against the Legitimists
and the bourgeoisie of the July Monarchy.
It was in 1840, a few months before the
Return of the Ashes, that Horace Vernet
delivered the painting to the engraver
Jazet so that it could be promulgated in
time for the ceremonies of the entomb-
ment of the Emperor's remains.

I

1769-1794

I

Napoleone Buonaparte

5

Jean-Baptiste-Claude-<u>Eugène</u> Guillaume
(1822–1905)

Napoleon Bonaparte in 1780

Musée national des châteaux
de Malmaison et Bois-Préau;
MM 40–47–6842;
Gift of Madame Henri Lefuel,
descendant of the sculptor
Plaster
H. 70; W. 45
Second Empire

This bust is one of a series of six sculptures portraying
Napoleon at different stages of his life: together with a
full-length statue, they once adorned the atrium of the
Pompeian villa erected by Prince Napoleon (1821–1891),
son of the former King Jérôme, on the Avenue Montaigne,
near the Champs-Élysées. The mansion, constructed
between 1856 and 1858 by architect Alfred Normand with
every antique detail restored, was sold in 1866 and
demolished in 1891. The series of marble sculptures was
completed in 1863 and shown at the Universal Exhibition
of 1867; after the demolition of the Pompeian villa they
were moved to the villa of Prangins, the Imperial family's
Swiss residence (the sculptures are now held by the
Napoleonmuseum, Arenenberg, Switzerland), while the
plaster models remained in the artist's studio.

As fate would have it, Napoleon was born in Ajaccio on August 15, 1769, just as the troops of King Louis XV of France were taking possession of Corsica. The future Emperor's father, Charles Bonaparte, was an influential lawyer in Ajaccio. In 1764 he married Letizia Ramolino, a girl of fourteen; there followed thirteen pregnancies before Charles died in 1785. He had used his French citizenship to obtain recognition of the Bonaparte family as noble and, taking advantage of the privileges of rank, enrolled young Napoleon first in the Military College at Brienne and then in the Royal Military College, Paris.

Some months after his father's death, on September 1, 1785, Napoleon was commissioned second lieutenant of artillery in La Fère's regiment, beginning a career as a soldier that would not end until the evening of June 18, 1815 on the plain of Waterloo. The monotony of garrison life led him to read voraciously; he wanted to know everything, and was passionately fond of natural history as well as universal history and geography. Nothing escaped him during those four years, as he learned about great empires — Athens, Rome, Byzantium — and great conquerors like Alexander, Hannibal and Julius Caesar. Making a list of British colonial possessions, he jotted down "St.Helena, small island"....

The early days of the revolution do not seem to have been of much concern to the young lieutenant, as he applied time and again for leave to go home to Corsica. He was, however, in Paris in the summer of 1792 and was present at the storming of the Tuileries by the mob, a sight he would recall with distaste. Meanwhile in his homeland the political situation had developed into a confrontation between supporters of integration into the French republic, represented by the Bonapartes and those around them, and proponents of a free Corsica; the latter were led by Paoli, who appealed to the English. In 1793 the Bonaparte home in Ajaccio was pillaged by the Paolists and the family forced to flee the island and take refuge in Marseilles. Napoleon was obliged to travel at once to Toulon, beseiged by the English. There he acquitted himself so brilliantly in the city's defence that he was made brigadier-general (December 1793) and also contracted scabies, a painful skin complaint that gave him the yellow-green complexion apparent in early portraits.

7

Léonard-Alexis Daligé de Fontenay
(1813–1892)

The Emperor Napoleon's Birthplace, Ajaccio

Musée national des châteaux
de Malmaison et Bois-Préau;
MM 40–47–7218;
Laussedat Bequest, 1929
Oil on canvas; signed, lower right
"A^{ls} de Fontenay (Corse)"
H. 38; W. 46
Salon de 1849, n° 740;
collection of Napoléon III;
sale of the Empress Eugénie
(3rd sale), 1927, n° 952.

Like all his brothers and sisters with the
exception of Joseph (who was born Corsican
but in Corte), Napoleon first saw the light
of day in the family house in the old city of
Ajaccio. Part of it had come into the
Bonaparte family through a marriage in
1682, but it was not until the late-eighteenth
century that they became owners of the
whole mansion. It was partly destroyed by
English troops in 1793, but completely
restored and refurbished by Napoleon's
mother between 1797 and 1799. He himself
last saw it after his return from Egypt, during
a short visit from September 29 to October 5,
1799. The house remained in the possession
of the Emperor's family until 1923, when it
was offered to the State by Prince Victor
Napoleon. In 1967 it was classed as one of
the national museums of France, linked with
the Musée de Malmaison.

6

Napoleon's cradle

Ajaccio, private collection
Walnut
H. 54; W. 110; L. 58
Beginning of the second-third of the 18th century (about 1765)

This traditional Corsican cradle was used for all Letizia Bonaparte's children including Napoleon. It then passed into the family of Charles Bonaparte's first cousin and brother-in-law Nicolo-Luiggi Paravicini (1739-1813), whose first wife had been Charles's sister. Gertrude Bonaparte died in 1793 in Pisa, where she had fled during the English occupation of Corsica. It was in the house, near Ajaccio, of this uncle by marriage that Napoleon found refuge in 1793 after the Bonaparte home was sacked. "Madame Mère" (My Lady Mother) then gave the cradle to Nicolo-Luiggi Paravicini's second wife Maria-Rosana Pô (1823) when her daughters were born. The cradle has remained in the family up to the present day.

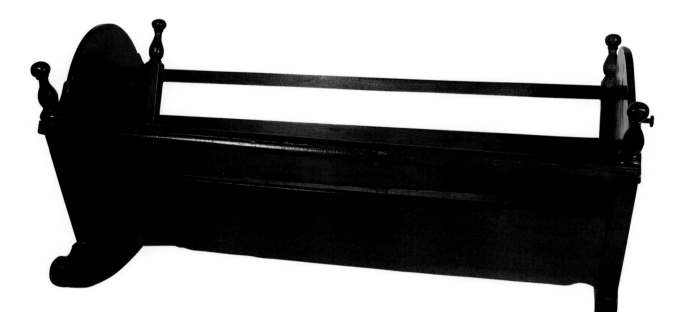

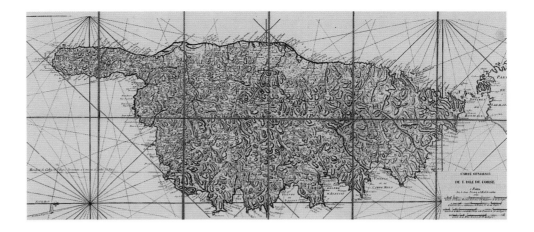

8
Jacques-Nicolas Bellin
(1703–1772)

Map of Corsica

Ajaccio, Musée national
de la Maison Bonaparte;
MNMB 70–2–1
Paper mounted on linen
H. 40; W. 85
1769

This map is from *The Quarto*
volume of the *Essais géographiques
sur la Corse*, published in Paris in
1769, the year of Napoleon's birth.
The mapmaker, Jacques-Nicolas
Bellin, worked in the Navy's charts
and plans department: he had
been appointed state surveyor and
ordered to chart all known coasts.
As Corsica was so badly administered by the Republic of Genoa,
France made various attempts over
the centuries to seize the island by
sending in troops (the first French
occupation took place in the reign
of Henri II (1553-1559). Despite
Pascal Paoli's efforts to establish
an independent state, the Treaty
of Paris, signed in 1768 between
Genoa and France ceded the
island to the latter, just a year
before the birth of that country's
future Emperor.

9
Carrara workshop,
after Antonio Canova
(1757–1822)

**Bust of Madame Mère, née Letizia Ramolino,
Napoleon's mother**

Musée national des châteaux
de Malmaison et Bois-Préau;
MM 40–47–6837;
Gift of Comte Joseph Primoli, great-grandson of Lucien
and Joseph Bonaparte
(the original statue shown at the Salon of 1808 is now
in the collection of the Duke of Devonshire at
Chatsworth House, England)
White marble
H. 58
About 1810

Letizia Ramolino, born in Ajaccio in 1749, was
descended from a family of the Tuscan nobility
that settled in Ajaccio in the late-15th century at
the same period as did the Bonapartes. Letizia was
only fourteen when in 1764 she married Charles-
Marie Bonaparte (1746-1785), a young law student
who was to end up as representative of the
Corsican nobility at the French court. The couple
had thirteen children, eight of whom survived.
Keeping calm in the face of her son's lightning
ascent to power, Letizia did not attend his
coronation, choosing to stay in Rome with her son
Lucien, who was at odds with Napoleon at the
time. Under the Empire she was given the title
"Her Imperial Highness the Mother of the
Emperor" and provided with substantial monies
which she never spent in their entirety; Letizia
thought always of the future, in her eyes an
uncertain one. Although she accompanied the
Emperor to the island of Elba, she was not
permitted to follow him into exile on St. Helena.
She retired to her house in Rome where she died
at last in 1836, having seen the deaths of three
of her children – Napoleon, Pauline and Elisa –
and of her granson, the Duc de Reichstadt.

10

Paolo Triscornia (+ 1832)
and Bartolomeo Franzoni, after
Joseph-Charles Marin (1759–1834)

**Bust of Charles-Marie Bonaparte,
Napoleon's father, executed posthumously**

New York, Malmaison Antiques Collection
White marble
H. 74.6
About 1810

From about the year 1200 the Bonapartes from
father to son were notaries in Sarzana, a small
town situated between Genoa and La Spezia. In
1490 one Francesco Bonaparte settled in Ajaccio
as a mercenary and founded a line of important
city officials known as the Ancients of Ajaccio.
In the second half of the 18th century the sole
remaining male heir was Carlo-Maria Buonaparte,
a proponent of Corsica's reunion with France
who began his career with elan. Charles de
Buonaparte, as he now began to call himself,
was called to the bar of the Upper Bench of
Corsica and appointed assessor of the Royal
Jurisdiction of Ajaccio. In 1771 he was granted his
letters patent of nobility by the King of France,
and in 1777 he was elected deputy for the nobility,
to represent Corsica at court, presenting himself
at Versailles the following year. Although impe-
cunious, he was able to place his children in the
royal military academy and the girls' school at
Saint-Cyr. Charles died prematurely in Montpellier,
where he had gone seeking a cure for an
advanced cancer.

11

Facsimile of Napoleon's baptismal certificate

Ajaccio, Musée national de la Maison Bonaparte;
unnumbered
Cardboard facsimile
H. 12; W. 22
Original: 1771

There exist two copies of Napoleon's baptismal
certificate, written in Italian: one is held in the
town archives of Ajaccio, the other in the depart-
mental archives of southern Corsica, held in
Ajaccio. The translation is as follows: "In the year
one thousand seven hundred and seventy-three,
on the twenty-first day of July, took place the holy
ceremony and the usual prayers for Napoleone, a
son born of the lawful marriage of Charles, son of
the late Joseph Bonaparte, and of Madame Marie-
Letizia his wife, who was christened in their home,
with permission, by the Very Reverend Lucien
Bonaparte, born on the fifteenth of August, 1769.
Present at the baptism were the most illustrious
Laurent Giubega, of Calvi, the King's Prosecutor,
as godfather and Madame Gertrude, wife to Sir
Nicolas Paravicino; the father being present, those
persons signed with me:
Jean-Baptiste Diamante, steward, Laurent
Giubega, Charles Bonaparte, Gertrude Paravicino."
Napoleon, aged two at the time, was christened
on the same day as Maria-Anna, who died at the
age of five months.

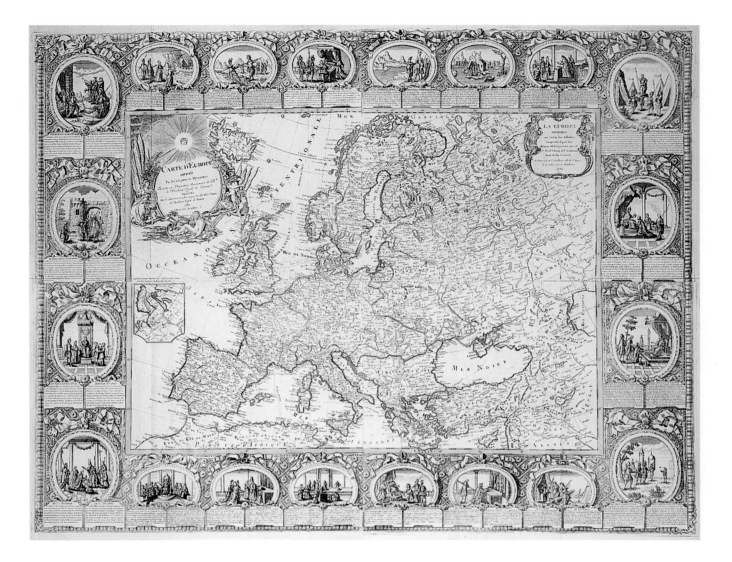

12

Abbé Clouet, cartographer
(1729 – ?)

Map of Europe, divided into its empires and kingdoms subjected to the astronomical scrutiny of the Gentlemen of the Royal Academy of Sciences. Drawn up from the most recent notes of the Reverend Abbé Clouet of the Académie de Rouen. 1782. [Published at] Paris by Mondhare

Montreal, The Stewart Museum at the Fort, Île Sainte-Hélène; inv. 1983.552
Line-engraving, embellished in colour
H. 99.7; L. 128
1782

This wall map of Europe is one of a set of five showing the world and the four continents. They were meant for the walls of studies and libraries, and are decorated with cartouches depicting the major historical events of each continent. This map bears on its periphery twenty cartouches depicting European history and legends. The notes to the illustrations are written in French and Spanish. Corsica's position in the Mediterranean is significant: the island lies much closer to Italy than to France.

G.V.

14

Louis Rochet
(1813–1878)

Napoleon Bonaparte, student at the École royale Militaire de Brienne, aged fifteen

Musée national des châteaux
de Malmaison et Bois-Préau
(Fonds Napoléon); N 424;
Purchase, 1979 (formerly the collections of
the Imperial family)
Silvered galvanized bronze executed
by the firm of Christofle
H. 172
1879, after the original plaster of 1853

In accordance with the wishes expressed by the Emperor at St. Helena, in 1853 Napoleon III granted the sum of 400,000 francs to the town of Brienne-le-Château, 25,000 of which were to raise a statue. The town council commissioned the work from the sculptor Rochet. The young Bonaparte is shown standing in his school uniform; in his left hand he holds a copy of Plutarch's *Lives of Great Men*, while his right hand is slipped into his waistcoat in the attitude to become so well-known after he became Emperor. The plaster model was exhibited at the Salon of 1853 and the bronze unveiled in Brienne in 1859. Many copies are extant, in plaster, marble and silvered bronze; this one was probably made for the Princess Mathilde, cousin to Napoléon III, and is now in the collection of the Imperial family.

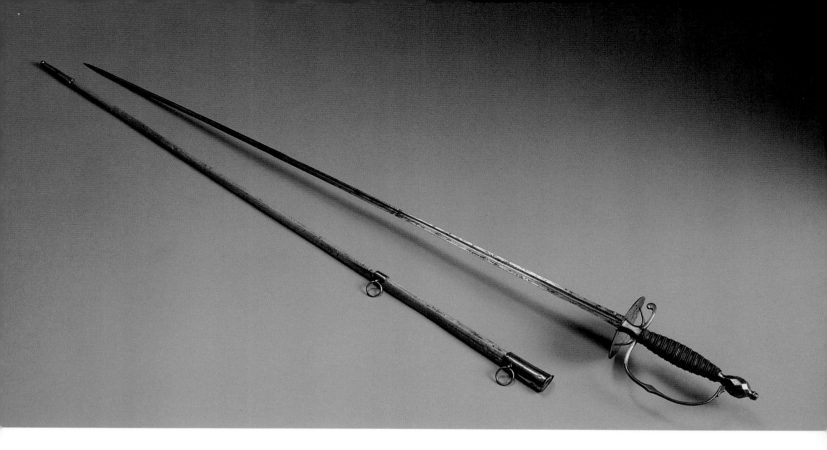

15

Lieutenant Napoleon Bonaparte's dress sword

Musée national des châteaux de Malmaison et Bois-Préau (Fonds Napoléon); N 194;
Purchase, 1979 (formerly the collections of the Imperial family)
Steel, copper, leather
L. 94
Late-18th century

This full-sized dress sword was worn by Bonaparte as a lieutenant. As Emperor he later
gave it to one of his pages, young Jules-Henri Duris-Dufresne (born in 1795), a nephew of
General Bertrand, his Grand Marshal of the Palace. In 1809 in his study at the Tuileries the
Emperor was chatting with a group that included General Bertrand and young Dufresne.
Napoleon questioned the latter on various military topics, and as the youth gave very
intelligent replies, took from a chest a sword with his own sash still attached and said to
Dufresne: "Here you are, my lad, take this sword that I wore when I was a lieutenant –
it will bring you luck". Lovingly preserved, it was later given to the Imperial family by
Madame Duris-Dufresne.

13

Napoleon Bonaparte's compass from the Royal Military School of Brienne

Musée national des châteaux de Malmaison et Bois-Préau (Fonds Napoléon); N 126;
Gift of T. I. H. Prince Napoleon Bonaparte and Countess de Witt, 1979
Wood, copper, leather, paper
L. 18.5; W. 16.5
About 1780

The young Bonaparte used this compass while at Brienne, and after becoming Emperor
gave it to Marie-Antoine de Reiset (1775-1836), a brigadier-general and baron of the Empire,
in 1813. De Reiset bequeathed it in 1828 to his nephew L. Blanchard, a cavalry officer, whose
son later gave it to the Emperor's family.

16

Officer's gorget

Montreal, The Stewart Museum at the Fort,
Île Sainte-Hélène;
inv. 1970.12
Gilded brass and silver-plate
H. 5.2; W. 12
France; about 1780

The gorget, a metal plate that protected the neck of
an armoured knight in the Middle Ages, became in a
smaller version one of the symbols of command worn
by army officers from the from the late-17th century
until the 19th century.
G.V..

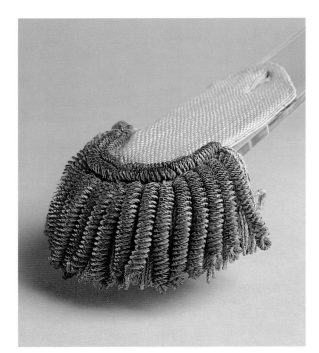

17

French officer's epaulettes

Montreal, The Stewart Museum at the Fort,
Île Sainte-Hélène;
inv. 1965.3
Cloth and silver thread
France; about 1780

The overhaul of the French army in 1762, carried out
under the direction of the Duc de Choiseul, introduced
the wearing of epaulettes as another distinguishing
feature of officers' uniforms. The rank and regiment
were indicated by the presence or absence of fringe,
the thickness of the slub and the colours.
G.V.

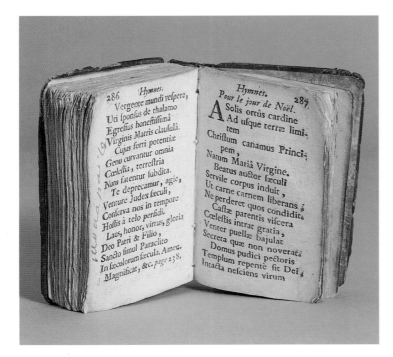

18

Napoleon's prayerbook from Brienne, entitled "Royal Hours" (the title page has disappeared)

Musée national des châteaux
de Malmaison et Bois-Préau
(Fonds Napoléon) N 437;
Gift of T. I. H. Prince and Princess Napoleon
Bonaparte, 1979
Calf, paper
H. 10.5; W. 7
Last third of the 18th century

Buonaparte used this prayerbook as a cadet at the Royal Military School at Brienne. The name "Buonaparte" has been written in ink in the margins of pages 104, 178 and 286.

19

After Jean-Baptiste Greuze
(1725–1805)

Captain Bonaparte aged twenty-two

Musée national des châteaux
de Malmaison et Bois-Préau;
MM 54–1–26; purchase, 1954
Colour print
H. 12.3; W. 10; page: H. 30.6; W. 21.3
19th century

In addition to this colour print, the Musée de Malmaison has several black and white prints of the portrait engraved by Auguste Blanchard (1792-1849). The original canvas (H. 56; L. 46; private collection) was painted by Greuze in 1792, while Bonaparte was in Paris just after being commissioned captain in the artillery. It was bequeathed to Caroline Greuze, the artist's daughter, and appeared in her sale of January 25 and 26, 1843; it then formed part of the Susse collection before being purchased by the Comte de Las Cases, author of the *Mémorial de Sainte-Hélène*.

20

C. de Last, after the painting by Francisque
Grenier de Saint-Martin
(1793–1867) painted in 1818

**Siege of Toulon: attack on the fortress
of Mont Faron (December 17, 1793)**

Musée national des châteaux
de Malmaison et Bois-Préau;
MM 58–2–269;
Gift of Princess George of Greece, 1958 (formerly the
Demidoff Collection, Prince de San Donato, passing to
Prince Roland Bonaparte, the donor's father)
Lithograph taken from *Victoires et Conquêtes
des Français*, volume 2, p. 155
H. 42; W. 57.8
1828–1829

The Republic, hoping to take back the city of
Toulon which had opened its gates to the English,
called in General Carteaux, a notoriously incom-
petent soldier. Young Captain Bonaparte took over
command of the artillery, even firing ordnance
himself. He was everywhere at once, had his horse
killed under him and was wounded in the thigh.
A final assault proved victorious, and the English
abandoned Toulon on December 18, 1793.
Bonaparte was immediately promoted to
brigadier-general at the age of only twenty-four.

22

**Neckerchief worn by Napoleon
Bonaparte at the siege of Toulon**

Musée national des châteaux
de Malmaison et Bois-Préau
(Fonds Napoléon) N 308;
Gift of T. I. H. Prince and Princess
Napoleon Bonaparte, 1979
Cotton
H. 65; W. 66
Late-18th century

This plain neckerchief worn by Captain
Bonaparte at the siege of Toulon has
been lovingly preserved. It is embroidered in cross-stitch with the initials
N B for Napoleon Bonaparte.

21

Belleyme, Pierre de, cartographer
(1747–1819) and Barrière, engraver
(possibly Barrière senior (1764–1823)

***Map of France, divided into 88 departments
and subdivided into districts with the chief
towns of the counties, presented to the
National Assembly.***

Montreal, The Stewart Museum at the Fort,
Île Sainte-Hélène; inv. 1999.4
Line-engraving, highlighted in colour,
glued on canvas
H. 161; W. 118
Paris; 1791

Corsica can be seen in a box that makes the
Isle of Beauty seem close to the French coast.
This map belonged to Étienne-Jacques
Macdonald, brigadier-general in 1793 and
major-general the next year, who went on to
become Marshal of the Empire in 1809.
G.V.

27

**Scale model of field cannon and limber, Gribeauval type 8,
on the scale of 1/8th**

Paris, Musée de l'Armée; inv. 0 200

After active service in Austria, Jean-Baptiste Vaquette de Gribeauval
(1715-1789) was recalled to France where he became inspector of artillery.
He is known for having completely modernised this service, bringing in
numerous modifications to the cannon, gun-carriages, harness and
casings. He equipped the field artillery with 4, 8 and 12-pounder field-
guns and 6-pound mortars, while the siege artillery was comprised
of 8, 12, 16 and 24-pounder cannnon, 8-pounder howitzers, 8, 10 and
12-pounder mortars and 15-pounder swivel guns. All these improvements
proved of the greatest use during the Revolutionary wars and were
maintained under the Empire and after the Restoration.

23

François-Pascal-Simon, Baron Gérard (1770–1837)

Portrait of Désirée Clary (1774–1860). A sculpted version of the bust in the large painting exhibited in the Salon of 1810 with the title *Portrait de H. H. the Princess de Ponte-Corvo, Princess Royal of Sweden*

Paris, Musée Marmottan-Claude Monet; inv. 1068
Oil on canvas
H. 63; W. 52
About 1810

Désirée Clary, born into a wealthy family of Marseilles merchants and at one time engaged to marry Napoleon, was the younger sister of Julie who was to marry Joseph Bonaparte, Napoleon's elder brother. The Emperor wrote to Joseph: "In a happy household, one of the two must give way to the other. You, Joseph, are indecisive by nature, and Désirée is the same, wheras Julie and I know what we want. You would do better to marry Julie." Joseph did so, but the Clarys felt less enthusiasm at the idea of a second Bonaparte marrying into the family. Désirée married, in 1798, General Bernadotte, a man with a brilliant future ahead of him. He was made Crown Prince of Sweden in 1810, and became king in 1818. Désirée, who was crowned Queen of Sweden only in 1829, was never completely at home in her new country.

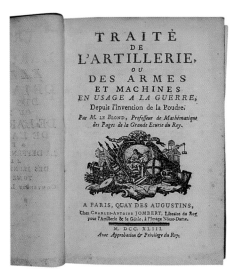

25

Guillaume Leblond (1704–1781)

Treatise on Artillery and the weapons and machines used in warfare since the discovery of gunpowder, by Monsieur Le Blond, professor of mathematics to the Pages of the King's Great Stable, Paris, Quay des Augustins, [published at] Paris by Antoine Jombert, Bookseller to the King for Artillery and engineering, at the sign of Notre-Dame, 1743

Montreal, The Stewart Museum at the Fort, Île Sainte-Hélène; 355/L49E/1743
Leather and paper
H. 25; W. 20; spine 2.5
Paris; 1743

This was one of many books in the collection of basic primers available to officer-cadets in the royal military schools when the young Napoleone Buonaparte was doing his training. *Emploi de l'artillerie nouvelle* (The Use of the New Artillery) by the Chevalier du Teil, published in 1778 and something new at the time, advocated concentrating artillery on the strategic targets likely to decide the victory.
G.V.

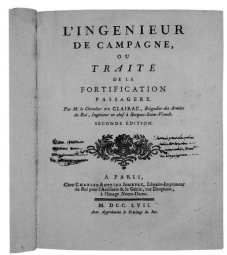

26

Louis-André de la Mamie de Clairac (about 1690–1750)

The Engineer in the Field or a Treatise on Temporary Fortifications, by the Chevalier de Clairac, Brigadier-General of the King's Armies and City Engineer for Bergues Saint-Vinock, Second edition, [published at] Paris by Charles Antoine Jombert, rue Dauphine at the sign of Notre-Dame, 1757

Montreal, The Stewart Museum at the Fort, Île Sainte-Hélène 355/C52/1757
Leather, paper
H. 25.7; W. 19.8; spine 4.5
Paris, 1757

Like the preceding volume, this was one of the "set books" for officer cadets of the royal military schools in Bonaparte's time.
G.V.

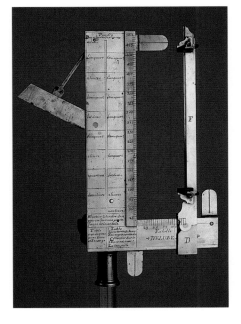

24

Delure, Paris

Twelve-inch mortar backsight

Montreal, The Stewart Museum at the Fort, Île Sainte-Hélène; inv. 1970.12.2
Brass
H. 12; W. 21
Mid-18th century

The mortar was a weapon with a specific purpose, developed by artillery engineers. Mortars were used to attack objectives hidden behind walls or by uneven terrain. Their high, curved trajectory made it possible during a siege to bombard the interior of a fortress. The calibre of a mortar is determined by the diameter of the shell (12 inches/30 cm). The backsight, mounted on a tripod and fixed in position by a ball-and-socket joint, was used to calculate the angle of fire in relation to the slope of the ground, and the amount of powder required to guarantee an effective shot at the required range. Three identical ordnance backsights made by Delure, the Paris manufacturers of scientific instruments, are extant. This is one of them.
G.V.

II

1795-1799

II

General Bonaparte

28

Jean-Baptiste-Claude-<u>Eugène</u> Guillaume
(1822–1905)

Napoleon Bonaparte in 1797

Musée national des châteaux
de Malmaison et Bois-Préau;
MM 40–47–6843;
Gift of Madame Henri Lefuel,
descendant of the sculptor
Plaster
H. 75; W. 70
Second Empire

This bust is another in the series
of six sculptures depicting Napoleon
at various points in his life.

After the fall of Robespierre (July 27, 1794), Napoleon was briefly harassed on account of his extremist Republican opinions, but in October 1795 he was thrust into the foreground of the political scene when he put down the royalist insurrection at the request of the Directory. It was at this moment, in Director Barras' salon, that he met General Beauharnais' widow and fell madly in love with her: Josephine stepped into Napoleon's life and into history. Without informing his family, the recently appointed General-in-chief of the Army of Italy married her on March 9, 1796 and left the next day to fight the Sardinians and the Austrians in Italy.

This first Italian campaign earned him the admiration of contemporaries. In eighteen days he beat the Sardinian army and turned to fight the Austrians, defeating them at Lodi, Arcola and Rivoli. Mantua surrendered on February 2, 1797, and Bonaparte pressed on to Vienna, where he forced the Emperor to capitulate and later to sign the peace agreement of Campo-Formio (October 17, 1797).

These astounding victories not only put France back among Europe's leading nations, but also made Bonaparte aware of his growing strength – he was awaiting his moment to seize power. There remained only one country to vanquish: England. His plan, a bold one, was not to attack her on her own soil but to carry the war into Egypt (then a Turkish possession) and thence to India to drive out the English. The members of the Directory were not unhappy to see the back of this over-ambitious young general, who had in their eyes become too popular. A fleet of 280 ships and 54,000 men left the port of Toulon for Egypt on May 19, 1798. The Battle of the Pyramids on July 21 of that year opened the gates of Cairo to Bonaparte, but on August 1 the French fleet was destroyed by Admiral Nelson in the harbour of Aboukir. Trapped by his conquests Bonaparte drove back the mighty Turkish army and, having subjugated the country, proceeded to reorganise it. Having brought with him numerous scholars, draughtsmen and artists, he established the Egyptian Institute to study the country: the geographical, scientific and above all the archae-ological publications that ensued were to open the way to modern Egypt.

36

Louis-Albert-Guislain, general,
Baron Bacler d'Albe
(1761–1824)

General Bonaparte

Musée national des châteaux
de Malmaison et Bois-Préau;
MM 40–47–7279;
Gift of Jacques Dubois-Chefdebien, 1942
Oil on canvas; signed, dated lower right:
"Br Dalbe A Milan/an V"
H. 55; W. 41
1796–1797

This is one of the two earliest known portraits
of Bonaparte, painted in Milan in year V
(September 1796 - September 1797) by Bacler
d'Albe, then official map-maker to the Army in
Italy before being put in charge of the Emperor's
topographical collection.

Two days after marrying Josephine, Napoleon
left Paris for Italy to strike at the Austrians before
marching on to Vienna. This campaign, admired
by strategists for its swiftness, enabled Bonaparte
to conquer the whole of northern Italy, threatening
the Pope and Austria sufficiently to force them to
make a separate peace. The victor emerged from
this gamble with a political advantage that neither
the Directory nor he himself had foreseen.

29

Gustave David (1824- after 1882), after Alfred de Marbot

Guards of the National Convention; plate from the *Galerie Militaire*
reproducing in 119 plates French costume between 1789 and 1815, and published in Paris
by Clément between 1856 and 1862

Montreal, the Stewart Museum at the Fort, Île Sainte-Hélène; inv. 1989.14
Lithograph
H. 44.7; W. 31
Second Empire

The Guard of the Convention, formed in the spring of 1793 to protect the nation's representatives,
was a standing force of only 500 soldiers whose job was to man various posts at the Tuileries
palace. Several of them were to attain high rank under the Empire: both Murat and Lefebvre
served in the guard. After the fall of Robespierre undesirables were weeded out, and Bonaparte
was able to call on a body of seasoned and disciplined troops when he had to defend the Convention against royalist insurgents on October 5, 1795 (year IV, 13 Vendemiaire in the Republican
calendar). By simply changing its name the Guard thus moved smoothly into the service of
the new regime with the title of Guard of the Directory.
G.V.

ATTAQUE DE LA CONVENTION NATIONALE ; JOURNÉE MÉMORABLE DU 13 VENDÉMIAIRE
An 4ᵐᵉ de la République Française.

30

Pierre-Gabriel Berthault (1737–1831), after Abraham Girardet (1764–1823)

Attack on the National Convention, the Memorable Day of the 13 Vendemiaire / year IV of the French Republic; plate n° 120 taken from the *Complete Collection of Historical Pictures of the French Revolution* published in five successive editions between 1791 and 1817

Montreal, The Stewart Museum at the Fort, Île Sainte-Hélène; inv. 1989.29
Line engraving
H. 24; W. 30.5; page: H. 28; W. 47.6
Between 1791 and 1817

The fall of Robespierre seemed to many to herald the end of the Revolution, but the Royalist party was still active and the Convention, threatened by a conspiracy, determined to save the situation by calling in the the troops. It was Barras, just appointed General of the Army of the Interior, who thought of bringing in young general Bonaparte, whose quick thinking saved the day. He had forty pieces of artillery brought from the Plaine des Sablons and without hesitation had the royalists gunned down on the steps of Saint-Roch Church on the 13 Vendemiaire an IV (October 5, 1795): the Republic was saved, and the nickname of "the Vendemiaire General" bestowed on Bonaparte, who received as recompense the generalship of the Army of the Interior while Barras became one of the five Directors of the new government, the Directory.
G.V.

31
Wedding basket given by Napoleon to Josephine
Musée national des châteaux de Malmaison et Bois-Préau (Fonds Napoléon);
N 393; Gift of T. I. H. Prince and Princess Napoleon Bonaparte, 1979
Silk, silver, copper, papier mâché
H. 44; W. 54; L. 30
1796

On the occasion of his wedding to Josephine in March 1796, Napoleon gave her this simple basket, known as a "sultan", which it was customary to decorate with fancy jewellery. It was regarded as a precious relic by the soon-to-be Emperor's family and remained in their collection until presented to the Musée de Malmaison in 1979. Made of unpretentious materials, it bears the letter J for Josephine; the Empress-to-be was christened Marie-Joseph-Rose but was called Rose until Napoleon decided to feminise her second name to Josephine: so Rose de Beauharnais became Josephine Bonaparte. In 1810, when the Emperor married again, he had made for Marie-Louise a wedding basket of vast size in wood and bronze which is now in the Glauco Lombardi Museum in Parma.

32
Ring given by Napoleon to Josephine, bearing the initials NB and the inscription "AMOUR SINCÈRE" (Sincere love)
Musée national des châteaux de Malmaison et Bois-Préau;
MMD 29 (from the Louvre Museum);
Gift of the Empress Eugenie to her physician Dr. Hugenschmidt, who gave it to the Louvre in 1930.
Gold, enamel
D. 2
About 1796

This marriage between two very different people was a surprise to their contemporaries. There is no doubt that Napoleon was at the time madly in love with Josephine, and also aware of what a catch she was. He believed her to be rich, and in his eyes she was a woman of influence – a viscountess under the old regime who had frequented the salons of the mighty, widow of a general of the Revolution who had been one of the leading lights of the Constituent Assembly. Josephine for her part recognised the young general's aspirations and needed a protector for her children; now thirty-three, she felt it was time to provide for the future by a simple civil marriage that could always be annulled if circumstances warranted. The marriage, arranged by the couple, enraged the Bonaparte family, as Napoleon had informed neither his mother nor his eldest brother Joseph, the real chiefs of the clan. There began a positive vendetta which ended only in 1809 with the divorce and the intruder's departure.

BONAPARTE — JOSÉPHINE
MARIÉS EN 1796

33

Anonymous (executed by a wounded army officer);
Paris, Mail, rue de Vaugirard

Bonaparte - Josephine / Married in 1796

Musée national des châteaux de Malmaison et Bois-Préau;
MM 40–47–6078;
Gift of the Comte de Cambacérès
H. 21.5; W. 23 (with frame: H. 34; W. 40)

Josephine and Napoleon met for the first time in the fall of 1795
at Director Barras' salons, where his victory over the royalist
insurgents had made the Corsican the hero of the hour. Smitten
by the charms of the former Viscountess de Beauharnais, he wrote
to her one fine January morning of 1796: "Seven in the morning:
I awake full of you. Your portrait and the intoxicating memory of
last night have given my senses no rest. Sweet, incomparable
Josephine, what a strange effect you have on my heart!" She,
without being actually in love, saw in the young general with
the bright future a mainstay for her children, Eugène and
Hortense, and finally decided to marry him. On March 2, 1796
Bonaparte was appointed General of the Army in Italy; his civil
marriage took place on March the ninth.

34

Copy of Napoleon's marriage certificate

Archives de Paris
Paper
H. 18; W. 24
1850

The two original copies having disappeared in 1871,
one in the fire at the Hôtel de Ville and the other in
the fire at the Palais de Justice, the certificate is known
only from copies made during the nineteenth century:
the one in the Archives de Paris was made on June 6,
1850. The wedding was held on March 9, 1796 in the
town hall of the 2nd arondissement of Paris, then
housed in the old Hôtel de Mondragon at 3 rue d'Antin
(the present site of the Banque Paribas). Everything
in the document is absurd, from the birthdate of
Josephine who lopped four years off her age by using
a deceased sister's birth certificate, to that of Napoleon
who aged more than a year by using his elder brother
Joseph's birth certificate. To crown it all, one of the
witnesses was not of age, being only nineteen, and
the mayor, who had gone home to bed because the
bride was late, was replaced by a commissioner who
had no right to marry anybody!

35

Letter from Napoleon to Josephine (photograph)

Original in the Archives nationales (France), 400 AP 6, vol I, n° 3
Paper
July 17, 1796

Only just married, Bonaparte left Paris to lead his army into Italy.
The passionate love he felt for Josephine expressed itself in ardent
letters that she did not answer. She finally decided to join him
in Italy, where she stayed for eighteen months. These love letters
owe their fame to the personality of the writer, who put his whole
heart into them, as in this example in which he says that "the
charms of the incomparable Josephine incessantly kindle a living,
burning flame in my heart and in my senses".

38

Louis-Albert-Guislain, general, Baron Bacler d'Albe (1761–1824)
Crossing the Po, below Piacenza, May 7, 1796
Vincennes, collection du ministre de la Défense, SHAT; inv. B 161
Gouache; signed and dated lower centre " Dalbe pinxit 1798 "
H. 44.5; W. 66.4
1798

In September 1796 Bonaparte took on to his staff the army's mapmaker and surveyor
Bacler d'Albe, a sensitive artist and brave soldier. Considered the best cartographer of
his time, he would be made Baron of the Empire on in 1810 and brigadier-general in 1813;
in March 1814 he was put in charge of the ordnance depot just before the Empire fell.

Having left Paris on March 11, 1796, Bonaparte, General of the Army in Italy, began his
campaign on April 12 with a first battle at Montenotte, and after wiping out the Piedmontese
signed an armistice with the king of Sardinia on April 28th. The second half of the campaign
was aimed at crushing the Austrians and conquering Lombardy. Bonaparte made haste
to get his troops across the Po below Piacenza to force the Austrian forces to fight on
the plain.

39

Louis-Albert-Guislain, general, Baron Bacler d'Albe (1761–1824)

Crossing the Bridge at Lodi, May 11, 1796

Vincennes, collection du ministre de la Défense, SHAT; inv. B 160
Gouache; signed and dated, lower centre: "Bataille de Lodi / Peint par B. Dalbe / 1797"
H. 44.5; W. 66.4
1797

On May 11 a single column of French grenadiers crossed the bridge at Lodi, which was defended by the Austrians. He had two pieces of artillery mounted in line with the 200-yard-long bridge and with a much smaller body of troops succeeded in routing the enemy. This victory brought him to the gates of Milan, which he entered as conqueror on May 15th.

With a view to immortalising his victories, Bonaparte formed the habit of appointing artists to follow the army into the field. The body of work thus produced, which continued to grow until the late-nineteenth century, constitutes one of the French Ministry of Defence's most important collections and is of inestimable value from both the artistic and the documentary point of view.

40

Pier-Giuseppe-Maria, called Joseph Bagetti (1764–1831)
View of Lonato, August 3, 1796
Vincennes, collection du ministre de la Défense, SHAT; inv. B 35
Watercolour
H. 52; W. 80
Late-18th – early-19th century

Since 1830, the topographic collection had been under the direction of General Baron Pelet.
However, he was forced to transfer many original water-colours to the history galleries
at Versailles being assembled by the King Louis-Philippe. In order to preserve the original
collection, he had copies made by the painters, Morel and Parent.

To liberate one of their divisions blockaded in Mantua, the Austrians confronted the French
but were defeated at the battles of Lonato (August 3th) and Castiglione (August 5th).

41

Pier-Giuseppe-Maria, called Joseph Bagetti (1764–1831)

View of the Battle of Arcole, November 17, 1796

Vincennes, collection du ministre de la Défense, SHAT; inv. B 40
Watercolour
H. 52; W. 79.5
1807

As a native of Turin, Bagetti was a subject of the King of Sardinia who appointed him court artist and landscape painter. He was freed from duty after the defeat of the Piedmontese in 1796, and entered Bonaparte's service officially, working at the War Depot. His many sketches made *in situ* were the basis for his watercolours, which set the standard for war artists of later generations. In 1816 Bagetti returned to his native Piedmont, where he died in obscurity.

In a third attempt to take Mantua, the Austrians sent in 50,000 men against Bonaparte's eighteen thousand. The French were in a sticky situation, but as the opposing troops were divided into two wings, Bonaparte in a tricky move concentrated his forces against only one of them. This was the famous episode immortalised by Gros in the painting of the young general, flag in hand, leading his grenadiers under a hail of bullets to cross the bridge at Arcole. In fact Bonaparte was jostled in the throng and fell into the marsh, from which he was with difficulty extracted.

42

Pier-Giuseppe-Maria, called Joseph Bagetti (1764–1831)
Crossing the Tagliamento, March 16, 1797
Vincennes, collection du ministre de la Défense, SHAT; inv. B 53
Watercolour
H. 52.5 ; W. 79.5
1807

Having failed to crush the French army, the Austrians launched a second offensive two
months later. Again taking advantage of the enemy's mistake in dividing up their forces,
Bonaparte concentrated his troops against the wing in the valley. This was the battle of
Rivoli; it began at four in the morning and ended that evening in victory for the French
and the headlong flight of the Austrians, who left behind 5,000 prisoners. Two weeks
later, with no resources left, Mantua was obliged to surrender.

43

Pier-Giuseppe-Maria, called Joseph Bagetti (1764–1831)

View of the Rivoli Basin between Mount Corona and Mount Pipolo, January 14, 1797

Vincennes, collection du ministre de la Défense, SHAT; inv. B 45
Watercolour with gouache highlights
H. 62; W. 101.5
Late-18th – early-19th century

With all his troops assembled, Bonaparte decided to march on Vienna. The Emperor of the
Holy Roman Empire entrusted his young brother the Archduke Charles with the task
of halting the French. Having crossed the river Piave, Bonaparte's army swept the Austrians
aside at the Tagliamento on March 16 and marched on victorious towards Vienna. It was
only after the French had reached Leoben, barely more than 20 miles from the capital, that
the Emperor agreed to sign the preliminary peace agreement (April 18, 1797) that would be
followed by the Treaty of Campo-Formio.

37

General's sash worn by Bonaparte during the Egyptian campaign

Musée national des châteaux de Malmaison et Bois-Préau
(Fonds Napoléon); N 288;
Gift of T. I. H. Prince Napoleon Bonaparte
and Countess de Witt, 1979
Wool, cashmere
W. 200; L. 60
About 1798

Bonaparte wore the uniform of a General of the Republic including a wide tricolour sash with a multicoloured cashmere border. On returning from Egypt he gave this sash, which he had worn during the campaign, to Hortense de Beauharnais, Josephine's daughter. It passed to her son, Napoleon III and then to Empress Eugénie, and remained in the Imperial family's collection until acquired by the Musée de Malmaison in 1979.

63

Anonymous, "[The firm of] Bonneville,
rue Jacques n° 195"

Arrival of Bonaparte in Egypt, General in Chief of the Army and Navy of the French Republic

Musée national des châteaux de Malmaison et Bois-Préau;
MM 40–47–4353
Coloured line-engraving
H. 26.3; W. 18.2; frame: H. 50.8; W. 38.8
Late-18th century

Bonaparte wore the uniform of a general of the Republic including a wide tricolour sash identical to the one shown here. In his left hand he holds the text of the speech he gave to his soldiers at Toulon ten days before the fleet sailed on May 9, 1798 (20 Floreal, year VI): "Officers and Soldiers. Know that you have not yet done enough for the Motherland... You will face new dangers, you will share them with our brothers the mariners... Their courage is as great as yours, their determination is to triumph, they will succeed in this with you... — Extract from Bonaparte's speech of the 20 Floreal, year VI of the Republic."

46

Dromedary saddle-cloth

Musée national des châteaux
de Malmaison et Bois-Préau;
MM 40–47–226
(from the Mobilier national)
Silk, cotton
W. 240; L. 150
Late-18th century

After pacifying Lower Egypt, the French
army had to march into Syria to face the
Turks, who were attempting to invade
that country. After some initial successes, they were stopped short at Acre
and were obliged to turn back towards
Aboukir to fight another Turkish army.
The situation was becoming almost
intolerable for Bonaparte, and the news
from Paris was far from reassuring.

The French army's use of dromedaries
made pack-saddles and saddle-cloths
necessary. After the Egyptian campaign
these camel-trappings were brought
back to France, where they have
remained in the national collections;
having never been used since that time,
most of the saddles are in a remarkably
good state of preservation.

45

Dromedary packsaddle

Musée national des châteaux
de Malmaison et Bois-Préau;
MM 40–47–227
(from the Mobilier national)
Wood, iron, copper
H. 48; W. 127
Late-19th century

48

Philippe-Joseph-Auguste Vallot
(1796–1840) after Antoine-Jean,
Baron Gros (1771–1835)

**Bonaparte before the Battle of the Pyramids
(July 21, 1798):
"Soldiers! From those monuments yonder,
forty centuries look down upon you"**

Musée national des châteaux
de Malmaison et Bois-Préau;
MM 58–3–36 bis;
Gift of Princess George of Greece, 1958
(formerly the Demidoff collection,
Prince de San Donato, later Prince Roland
Bonaparte, the donor's father)
Line-engraving
H. 76; W. 54
1838

This print reproducing the famous painting
by Gros which Napoleon commissioned
in 1809 for the conservative Senate (the
Luxembourg Palace) was shown at the Salon
of 1810 and found its way to the Versailles
museum in the reign of King Louis-Philippe
(inv. MV 1496). The painting depicts the famous
scene of Bonaparte's speech to his soldiers as
he gestured towards the pyramids: "Onward,
and remember that from those monuments
yonder, forty centuries are watching us", which
the nineteenth century would rephrase as
"From the Pyramids yonder, forty centuries
look down on you." The 6,000 Mamelukes
were defeated, with losses of over 1,500 men.
Murad Bey fled to Upper Egypt, and Ibrahim
Bey retreated to Syria. This victory took the
French into Cairo the following day, on July 22nd.

49

Claude Chappe
(1763–1805)

Telegraph message announcing the victory at Aboukir

Île d'Aix, Musée national de l'île d'Aix;
MG. A.434; Baroness Napoleon Gourgaud
Bequest (*née* Eva Gebhard) 1959.
Printed form signed "Chappe. Certified as true,
administratior for the Lower Rhine, Christiani"
H. 44; W. 37
1799

Abbé Claude Chappe (1763-1805), a physics and mechanical engineering enthusiast, presented to the Legislative Assembly in 1792 a system of rapid communication by means of visual signals. Together with his four brothers he was authorised by the government to construct the first telegraph line between Paris and Lille; it was completed in August 1794. It had become possible through these telegraph lines to transmit all kinds of messages over long distances with a numbered vocabulary of 9,000 words. Telegraph stations set up every two to three leagues (about 5 to 8 miles) took only a few minutes to send an express from Lyons to Paris. This was not the case, however, in Egypt: the battle of the Nile was won at Aboukir on July 23, 1799, but it was not until October 9 that Chappe announced the news in Strasbourg (which is why the message is written in French and in German).

> # TRANSMISSION
> ## TÉLÉGRAPHIQUE
> ### DE PARIS A STRASBOURG.
> Le 17 Vendémiaire, an VIII.
>
> L'ARMÉE d'Orient a remporté une nouvelle victoire le 7 thermidor : elle a battu l'ennemi qui était parvenu à effectuer un débarquement à Abouckir; elle a tué ou noyé plus de six mille hommes, pris un grand nombre de drapeaux, quarante canons, tous les bagages et le Général qui commandait les Turcs.
>
> Signé CHAPPE.
> *Certifié conforme,*
> Le Commissaire central du Bas-Rhin, CHRISTIANI.
>
> ---
>
> ## Telegraphischer Bericht
> ### von Paris nach Straßburg.
> Vom 17ten Vendemiár Abends, im VIIIten Jahre.
>
> Die Morgenländische Armee hat den 7ten Thermidor einen neuen Sieg erfochten, und den Feind, welchem es gelungen war bey Abouckir zu landen, geschlagen. Mehr als sechs tausend Mann wurden getödtet oder ins Meer gesprengt; eine große Menge Fahnen, vierzig Kanonen und das ganze Kriegs-Geräthe fiel in unsere Hände, wie auch der General der die Türken anführte.
>
> Unterschrieben Chappe.
> Dem Original gleichlautend;
> Der Central-Kommissär des Nieder-Rheins, Christiani.

44

Bonaparte's sabre from the Egyptian campaign, marked Aboukir - Pyramides

Musée national des châteaux de Malmaison et Bois-Préau (Fonds Napoléon);
N 198; Purchase, 1979 (formerly the collection of the Imperial family)
Wood, gilded copper, velvet
W. 80
About 1798

Faced with the impossibility of invading England, Bonaparte planned to attack the English in India, first taking possession of Egypt as a useful replacement for France's lost colonies. In reality the ambitious young general was determined to win additional glory from this campaign while he awaited the collapse of the Directory, which would enable him to seize power in France. The 54,000 men of the Army in Egypt sailed from Toulon on May 19, 1798 and landed in Alexandria; beside the Pyramids they swiftly defeated the Mamelukes, the feudal ruling class whose authority was irksome to the Egyptian populace. Admiral Nelson's destruction of the French fleet in the harbour of Aboukir trapped the French army in the country Bonaparte planned to conquer.

In the course of the campaign Bonaparte wore various different sabres; some of them, of Oriental provenance, were presented to him by his staff. This one bears the inscriptions Aboukir and Pyramides.

47

Michele Rigo (1770–1814)

Sheikh Khalil al-Bakrî

Versailles, Musée national du château
de Versailles; inv. MV6835
Oil on canvas
H. 85; W. 63
1813

From a series of seven sketches
made during the campaign in Egypt
(Paris, private collection), the artist
Michele Rigo executed for Bonaparte
at Malmaison an initial series of six
portraits of sheikhs allied to France
(Musée de Malmaison). Three other
series were commissioned from the
artist by members of the expeditionary
force. They varied in price: Eugène de
Beauharnais paid 3,000 francs for his
(now in the German ambassador's Paris
residence), Berthier 2,400 F (now at the
Château de Grosbois) and Bessières
only 2,000 francs (his portraits are now
scattered). In 1813 a fifth and last series
was offered for sale by the artist at
2,000 francs and was purchased for the
great hall of Le Butard, the Emperor's
hunting lodge situated between
Malmaison and Versailles; the format
of the canvases, originally oval, was
changed when they were acquired by
the Musée de Versailles in the reign
of King Louis-Philippe. Sheikh Khalil
al-Bakrî, a member of the great *diwan*
of Cairo, died in 1809.

55

Document written in Arabic and French signed by Bonaparte

Private collection
Paper, signed Bonaparte
H. 35; W. 25
7 Pluviose Year VII (January 26, 1799)

Once established in Egypt, the French set about restoring order as a
primary concern. To do this, Bonaparte imposed a stringent organisa-
tional system and himself countersigned innumerable documents on
every kind of subject, most of them bilingual, written in Arabic and
French. This paper is a petition from coffee merchants complaining
about the functionaries bearing mandates and summonses from
Ibrahim Bey. To obtain further information on the matter, Bonaparte
ordered a report to be submitted to him, and sent the petition to
the Trade Tribunal.

50
Desouches, blacksmith
Camp bed
Musée national des châteaux de Malmaison et Bois-préau;
MM 40–47–2994;
Gift of Mr. And Mrs. Edward Tuck, 1911
Iron, copper, canvas
H. 108; W. 182; L. 86
About 1810–1814

From the days of his Consulate on, the blacksmith
Desouches made for Napoleon folding iron camp
beds with canvas strapping which he used for all his
campaigns; there was a small version, like this one,
that could be carried by pack-mule, or the large model
that was transported by wagon. Napoleon found
this simple camp bed so much to his liking that he
had one permanently set up in his small bedroom at
Fontainebleau. He took several of them with him
to St. Helena, and it was in a bed like this (now in the
musée de l'Armée) that he breathed his last.
The bed shown here was brought back from
St. Helena by Marshal Bertrand.

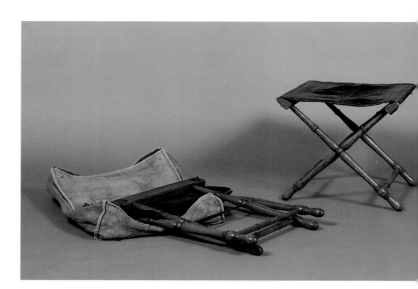

52
François-Honoré-Georges Jacob-Desmalter
(1770–1841)
Two folding campstools
Paris, Mobilier national; GMT 2424
Beechwood, iron, canvas, cotton, green Morocco leather
H. 45; L. 49; W. 48
About 1810

51

François-Honoré-Georges Jacob-Desmalter
(1770–1841)

Camp chair

Paris, Mobilier national; GMT 2427
Beechwood, iron, canvas, cotton, green Morocco leather
H. 87; L. 41; W. 40
About 1810

53

François-Honoré-Georges Jacob-Desmalter (1770–1841)

Camp table

Paris, Mobilier national; GMT 952
Cottonwood, walnut, iron
H. 70; L. 74; W. 47
About 1810

Among the striped twill tents put up on campaign there was the Emperor's two-room tent: in the first room, used as an office, were one or more folding tables on which to spread maps, an armchair reserved for the Emperor and several folding chairs, including two for his secretary and his aide-de-camp.

The second room was the bedroom, which held the famous little iron bed with the green silk curtains. All this furniture could be easily folded up to go into big leather sacks carried on mule-back. Extremely simple and very sturdy, these pieces of furniture were also used by King Louis-Philippe's sons during the campaign in Algeria.

54

Chayette et Cheval,
manufacturers, Paris

Box of draughtsman's tools
Montreal, The Stewart Museum
at the Fort, Île Sainte-Hélène;
inv. 1997.25
Wood, brass, iron, cloth
L. 21.2; W. 20.2
About 1774–1784

This splendid box of
drawing implements may well
have been used by a number of the
French scholars embarked on a scientific study of Egypt.
These implements – a ruler, a set-square, a proportional
compass, dividers, protractors and a pen – in the hands of
a scholar or trained engineer were used to draw up city plans,
charts and maps among other things. The masterpiece produced
by Napoleon's team was the monumental work entitled
Description of Egypt: the maps were drawn up by seven surveyors,
thirteen military and twelve civil engineers, two apprentice
engineers and three generals. These maps in fact ushered in
the age of modern cartography, providing as they did precise
indications of the siting of natural resources, communication
routes, demographics and economic activity. They were regarded
as a state secret at the time and were not made public until 1814.
J.F.G.

56

Charles-Louis Balzac (1752–1820), draughtsman, Paris;
etcher Pierre-Gabriel Berthault (1737–1831)

Edfu (Apollinopolis Magna) Overall View
Musée national des châteaux de Malmaison et Bois-Préau; MM 1117
(library inventory), Antiquités vol.1, pl. 48
Engraving on paper
H. 70; W. 55
Early 19th century

Before leaving to campaign in Egypt, Bonaparte decided to
add to the army a commission on the arts and sciences made
up of experts in all the fields that would confer the status of
scientific enquiry on the expedition. From 1798 to 1801 these
scholars collected all information relevant to geography, commerce,
agriculture and above all to understanding Egypt's ancient
monuments. The *Description of Egypt* came out in instalments
between 1809 and 1813 and then from 1818 to 1828, and consists
of: six volumes of *Antiquities Reports*; ten volumes of The *Modern
State*; six volumes of *Natural History*; and 900 engravings. The
work constitutes an irreplaceable source of information on the
country and its archaeology. The Musée de Malmaison possesses
the first three tomes, the only ones published under the Empire,
in a magnificent binding with the coat-of-arms of Napoleon I,
from the Imperial library, as well as a less sumptuous edition in
a cardboard binding and another, unbound copy from which
this plate was taken. This idealised view of the temple of Horus
at Edfu does not show what the expedition members saw.
The temple was then partially buried in sand and covered by
haphazard later building; it was cleared only in the 1860s
by the Frenchman Mariette.

58

Jesse Ramsden
(1735–1800)

Sextant

Montreal, The Stewart Museum at the Fort, Île Sainte-Hélène;
inv. 1989.19
Wood, brass, glass
H. 29.5; W. 32
London, England; about 1780–1800

The sextant, an instrument of navigation developed in the second half
of the 18th century, measures the angular distance of the stars by night
and the sun by day (hence the smoked glass for daylight) to determine
the latitude of the place from which the observation is taken. This
English-made sextant, precise to within 15 seconds of arc (about 0.06 of
a degree) is the work of a distinguished Fellow of the Royal Society,
Jesse Ramsden, and is a fine example of the meticulous craftsmanship
coming out of England. A sextant like this one was almost certainly
to be found in the baggage of at least one of the 160 scholars of
the Commission for Science and the Arts formed expressly for the
Egyptian campaign. It is, however, highly unlikely given the state
of war between England and France that General Caffarelli, in charge
of purchasing scientific instruments for the Commission's scholars
during their time in Africa, would have bought English instruments
for this collection, which was evaluated at 79,639 pounds and 70 sols.
By the end of the century, indeed, the Hexagon had craftsmen such
as Jean-Charles Borda and Étienne Lenoir who had nothing to fear
from competitors across the Channel.
J.F.G.

57

Lennel
(+1784), Paris

Graphometer

Montreal, The Stewart Museum at the Fort,
Île Sainte-Hélène; inv. 1970.4
Brass, glass
H. 9.5; W. 13.9
Paris; 1777

The maker of scientific instruments who signed
himself "Lennel at the sign of La Sphère, Paris,
1777" was active mainly between 1774 and 1784,
the year of his death. At that time London was
way ahead of France in the manufacture of precision instruments for the sciences. This state of
affairs can be seen in a treatise by the celebrated
astronomer Jérôme de Lalande entitled *Astronomie*,
which lists instruments, toolmakers and prices
current at the time. The list shows English
craftsmen so dominant in the field of precision-
instrument making that, in Lalande's own words,
they constituted "a monopoly that fills the French
with indignation". However, for instruments
requiring less precision, such as draughtsman's
implements, sundials and surveying tools like this
graphometer, the quality of French products was
equal to that of their neighbours across the
Channel. This instrument, together with a compass
and a vernier scale, was designed by Philippe
Danfrie in the late-16th century to calculate the
angle of the horizon between two distant
objects. Graphometers were found in all
military institutions, and the young Bonaparte
undoubtedly learned how to use one while a
cadet at the Brienne Military College (1779-1784)
and at the Royal Military College in Paris (1784-1785).
J.F.G.

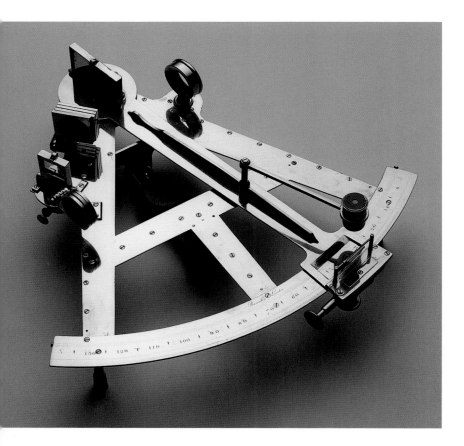

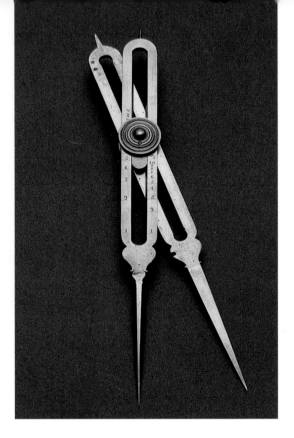

59
Anonymous (England)
Proportional compass
Montreal, The Stewart Museum at the Fort,
Île Sainte-Hélène; inv. 1998.7
Brass, steel
H. 29.5; W. 32
Late-18th century

The proportional compass makes it easy to recopy drawings of all sorts in various dimensions. This compass consists of four distinct scales: *lines*, *plans*, *solids* and *circles*. Each of the first three scales multiplies (or divides depending on the side used) a measurement by a whole number between 1 and 10. A straight line can quickly be tripled or divided by three and at the same time, if the line is the radius of a circle, do the same with the circumference of the circle with the minimum of effort. The same logic applies for plans and solids, except that in those cases two- and three-dimensional figures must be measured. The last scale, for circles, gives at once, without need for mathematical calculation, the dimensions of the edges of a polygon of six to twenty sides within a circle of a given radius. A proportional compass was essential to draughtsmen and engineers for speedy reproduction of drawings, whether maps or designs for buildings.
J.F.G.

60
Anonymous (France)
Table telescope
Montreal, The Stewart Museum at the Fort, Île Sainte-Hélène;
inv. 1998.10
Brass
H. 31. Lens 27
18th century

This Gregorian-type telescope with a folding tripod for transport had many uses for the astronomer. For example, the astronomer-engineer-geographer Nicolas-Auguste Nouet (1740-1811), one of the earliest members of the Commission for Science and the Arts appointed to the Egyptian Institute (mathematics section), used a telescope, not necessarily like this one, to observe the satellites of Jupiter. He used these observations to determine the longitude of several places west of the Nile delta. Although latitude could easily be calculated with a sextant, this was not the case for longitude. By observing from Egypt the eclipse of Jupiter's moons, regular foreseeable events forecast in the astronomical tables, Nouet could find the longitude of the place where he stood by calculating the time difference between his observations and the data provided by the tables for a fixed meridian. On returning to France he took up again the position he had held before leaving for Egypt as Director of Surveys for the map of Mont-Blanc in the Savoie. It was possibly for just this sort of work that the conversion ruler seen here, signed Billiet and once owned by d'Alexandry, was intended.
J.F.G.

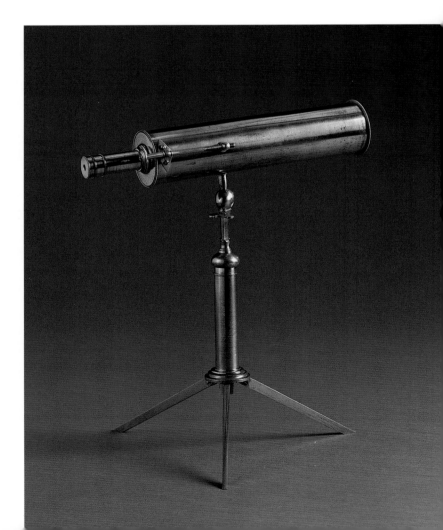

61

Anonymous (France)

Compound microscope

Montreal, The Stewart Museum at the Fort, Île Sainte-Hélène; inv. 1998.13
Mahogany, brass, steel, glass
Case: H. 16.5; W. 17.5. Lens 19
Microscope: H. 17.3; W. 36; L. 14.7
Paris?, France; late-18th century

The composite microscope, unlike the simple microscope, is made up
of at least two lenses. For purposes of observation, light is transmitted
by a concave mirror inside the casing; the light intensity is adjusted
by means of a perforated disc with four openings of different diam-
eters set into the casing. In the drawer can be seen a series of lenses
for enlarging the image together with specimen foceps, a small glass
burette for examining fluids and a magnifying glass. During the
Egyptian campaign numbers of biologists, botanists, zoologists and
mineralogists, members of the Egyptian Institute, studied the country.
Both Marie-Jules-César Savigny (1777-1851) who studied the insects of
Lower Egypt and Étienne Geoffroy Saint-Hilaire (1772-1844) could not
have arrived at their brilliant ichthyological analyses without the use
of a microscope. After the blockade of Alexandria in Thermidor IX
(late July 1801) Saint-Hilaire's passionate commitment to zoological
research produced important studies on the morphology and
classification of fish.
J.F.G.

62

Billiet

**Conversion ruler, once the property
of R. d'Alexandry**

Montreal, The Stewart Museum at the Fort,
Île Sainte-Hélène; inv. 1998.15
Brass
W. 19.5; L. 4.5
France (Savoie); 1792–1815

This conversion ruler, once the property of the
Savoy family d'Alexandry d'Orengiani, is a beautiful
example of the transition period in France following the decree of March 1791 (in the midst of the
French Revolution) that put in place the decimal
metric system. For the new Republic this uniformi-
sation of units of weight and measure was a
scientific issue and also a political one; the Jacobins
made the metre a weapon in their ideological
battle to unify the Republic. Seen from this view-
point the implementation of the metric system
in France testifies as much to the mathematical
mindset of the Enlightenment as to a "hatred for
kings". But in the provinces it was hard to change
the traditional units of measure. On this ruler the
"Savoie fathom" (about six French feet, or almost
two metres), the "Trabuc" (the French perch,
equivalent to 0.01 of an acre) and the rarely used
"Chambre half-foot" are found beside the metres
and decimetres. It would take no less than half
a century to put the reform in place throughout
France. The birthplace and career of the ruler's
maker Billiet are still unknown.
J.F.G.

III

1799-1804

III

First Consul

64

Jean-Baptiste-Claude-<u>Eugène</u> Guillaume
(1822–1905)

Napoleon Bonaparte in 1801
Musée national des châteaux
de Malmaison et Bois-Préau;
MM 40–47–6844;
Gift of Mme Henri Lefuel,
descendant of the sculptor
Plaster
H. 75; W. 52
Second Empire

This bust is one of a series
of six sculptures portraying
Bonaparte at different stages
of his life.

The news from France was alarming. Bonaparte decided to leave General Kleber and on August 23, 1799 he secretly embarked for France, landing on October 9th. In Paris the power he sought was there for the taking, and he seized it at Saint-Cloud on the night of November 9-10, 1799 (coup d'état of the 18 Brumaire). The new constitution provided for the appointment of three Consuls, of whom the first – Bonaparte – in fact held the real power. A few days after the referendum he moved into the Tuileries palace: Napoleon was becoming Bonaparte.

He immediately set about reorganising the administration and judiciary of France: he put government-appointed prefects at the head of the departments or administrative areas, organised the creation of the Banque de France (the only one authorised to issue banknotes), and established the franc, which was to remain stable for over a century. But as Austria and England turned down his peace proposals, he decided on an offensive in northern Italy and boldly led his troops over the Great Saint Bernard Pass. This imaginative stroke brought the army down into the valley of the Po, where it overwhelmed the Austrians at Marengo on June 14, 1800. The Emperor of Austria signed the Treaty of Lunéville (February 9, 1801), and Europe had peace at last.

It was now essential to restore peace at home through an astute policy of national reconciliation. Bonaparte therefore approached the Vatican to put an end to the schism that had split France since the Revolution, and after delicate negotiations, the Concordat was signed on July 15, 1801. He pursued his reforms, proposing a broad amnesty for émigrés on April 1802 and the following month reorganising the education system by establishing high schools. During the same period Bonaparte created a national order, the Legion of Honour, to reward both miltary and civilian merit. But the great achievement of his Consulate remains the Civil Code, later to be called the Napoleonic Code, the establishment of a body of law aimed at determining the relationships between individuals and especially conditions involving the family.

By the plebiscite of August 2, 1802, the nation voted Bonaparte Consul for life: the government of the Republic was now only a monarchy in disguise. The Peace of Amiens signed with England on March 25, 1802 confirmed his power both at home and abroad.

Throughout this period the real danger lay in the royalists' refusal to recognise the new power and their hope that the First Consul would place on the throne of their ancestors the Comte de Provence, whom they recognised as King Louis XVIII. Disappointed in this hope, they fermented several plots and even made unsuccessful attempts on Napoleon's life (the attack in the Rue Saint-Nicaise, December 24, 1801 and the Cadoudal conspiracy of May 1804). The conspirators were awaiting the arrival of a French prince, so the accidental presence of the Duc d'Enghien near the border doomed him in the eyes of Bonaparte, who had him kidnapped and later executed in the courtyard of the Chateau de Vincennes after a mockery of a trial. This was the final break with the royalists.

76

Jean-Baptiste Mauzaisse
(1784–1844)

**Napoleon Ist Crowned by Time
writes the Civil Code**

Musée national des châteaux
de Malmaison et Bois-Préau;
MM 40–47–8401;
Gift of Dr. Hugenschmidt
Oil on canvas; signed, upper left:
"Mauzaisse"
H. 131; W. 160
Salon of 1833

Before the Revolution life in France was
governed by many laws and edicts that
could give rise to as many divergent rulings.
The achievement of the Napoleonic Code
was to bring together all these laws in a
single text written in a clear and precise
manner. It still applies to a great extent in
Belgium and Luxembourg, and has also
influenced civil law in a number of other
European countries including Holland,
Germany, Switzerland and Italy. The swift
compilation of this huge body of law was
entirely Napoleon's doing; this imperishable
achievement stands as his alone.

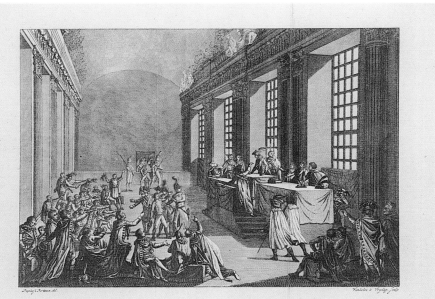

Zitting der wetgevinge te St Cloud, op den 9den en 10den van Slachtmaand 1799.

67

Vinheles and Vrydag after Jean Duplessis-Bertaux
(1747–1818)

Zitting der wetgevinge te St Cloud, op den 9den en 10den van Slachtmaand 1799: sitting of the Assembly at St Cloud, November 9 and 10, 1799, coup d'état of the 18 et 19 Brumaire year VIII (Dutch engraving)
Musée national des châteaux de Malmaison et Bois-Préau;
MM 40–47–1115;
Gift of M. de Contenson
Etching in bistre
Page: H. 21.8; W. 27.7
About 1800

After the resounding victory at Aboukir, Egypt, Bonaparte decided to return to France. Leaving his army behind, he arrived in Paris on the morning of October 16 determined to overthrow the five-Director government to his own advantage. A skilful publicity campaign presented him to the people as the saviour of the Republic, and once he had gained the support of most of the influential men in politics, he had only to circumvent the parliamentarians. This was done on November 10 when the two houses were assembled in the orangery of the Château de Saint-Cloud. The resistance put up by some deputies and the attempt to capture Bonaparte himself made the latter decide to send in the troops to clear the room; in their headlong flight a few deputies jumped out of windows, flinging off their scarlet togas so as to run faster. The following day the Consulate replaced the Directory.

68

Joseph Pel (20th century) after
Jean-Auguste-Dominique Ingres
(1780–1867)

Napoleon Bonaparte, First Consul
Musée national des châteaux
de Malmaison et Bois-Préau;
MM 40–47–2106;
Gift of the artist, 1929.
Oil on canvas; signed and dated, lower right:
"Joseph Pel-1929, after Ingres, Musée de Liège"
H. 220; W. 120
1929

The original of this painting was one of a series of canvases commissioned by Bonaparte from several artists to send to the main cities of Belgium. The young Ingres received 3,000 francs for this portrait, which was given to the city of Liège; he was allowed only one short sitting. The open curtain shows on the right the ancient cathedral of Saint-Lambert and the citadel of Sainte-Walburge. Bonaparte's hand on the document entitled "Amercœur suburb rebuilt" is an allusion to the decree of August 2, 1803 by which he had granted 300,000 francs for the reconstruction of this suburb of Liège, which had been bombarded by the Austrians in 1794. The red suit worn by the First Consul in this portrait no longer exists, and should not be confused with the suit in this exhibition.

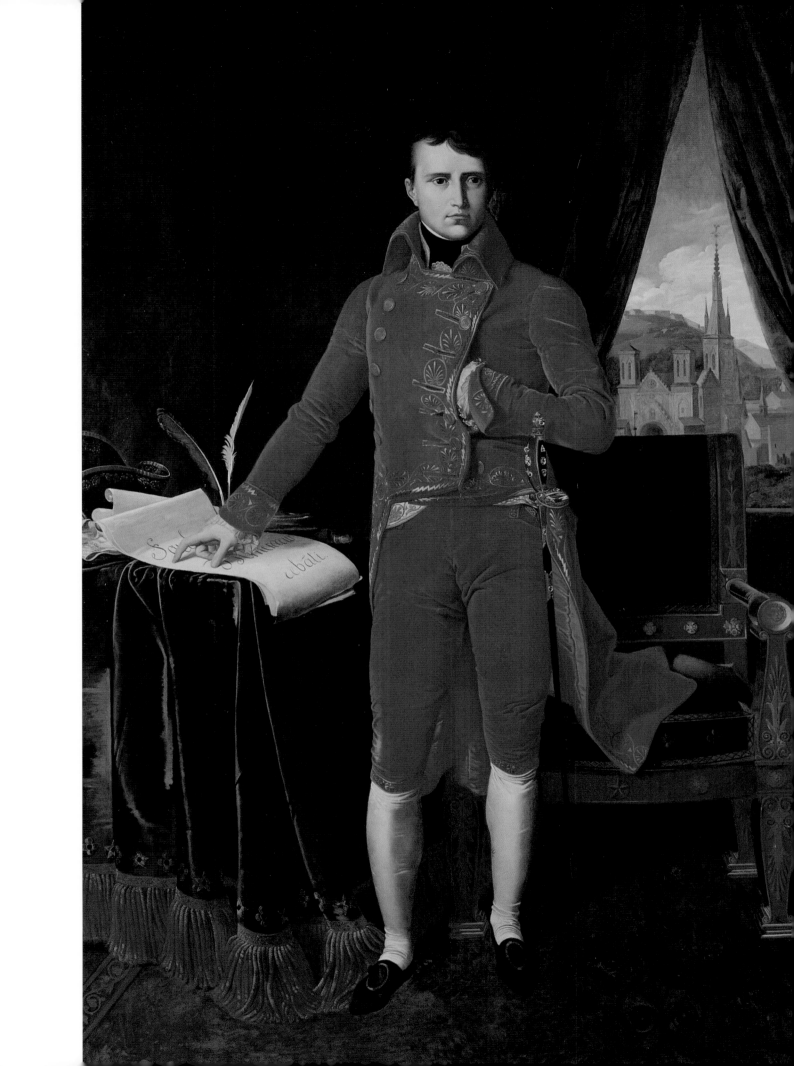

66

Christian-Friedrich Müller (1782–1816)

The Reserves Crossing the Alps by the Great St. Bernard Pass - le 24- Floréal year of the Republic (May 14, 1800)

Musée national des châteaux de Malmaison et Bois-Préau; MM 52–2–1;
Purchase, 1952
Pen and sepia ink wash
H. 37; W. 50
First Empire

Masséna's critical situation in Italy forced the First Consul to bring in his reserve army into the field as quickly as he could; time was of the essence, and he had to take the shortest but most difficult route. The ascent of the Great St. Bernard Pass over the Alps began on May 14, 1800. Bonaparte wrote to the consuls back in Paris: "We are contending with snow, ice, storms and avalanches. The St. Bernard, astonished at seeing so many people crossing in such a hurry, is putting some obstacles in our way. In three days the whole army will have crossed." Thus, in a bold move that the French press would compare to Hannibal's exploit, Bonaparte managed to get his army across the Alps to face the Austrians.

This is a preparatory sketch for plate I of the *Fastes Militaires de la France*, engraved by Helland.

BATAILLE DE MARENGO.

65

Antoine-Charles-Horace, called Carle Vernet (1758–1835)

Battle of Marengo

Musée national des châteaux de Malmaison et Bois-Préau; MM 66–9–1;
Gift of Mme Hector Lefuel and her children, 1966
Graphite, watercolour and gouache highlights on ivory paper
H. 56.5; W. 42.5
About 1805

On June 14, 1800 while seeking to confront the Austrian army Bonaparte let himself be
surprised by the enemy offensive. By afternoon the battle seemed lost, with the French
army retreating in good order from the less than eager pursuit of the Austrians. The arrival
of Desaix (soon, alas, to fall with a bullet in the heart) enabled Bonaparte to turn the situation
to his advantage and wrest a splendid victory from the jaws of defeat. The Minister of War,
Alexandre Berthier, wrote an "Account of the Battle of Marengo", printed in 1804 in a limited
edition. The handsomest edition of the text was presented to the Emperor on June 14, 1805,
the fifth anniversary of the battle, on the very site of the action, with 30,000 soldiers re-enacting
the combat under the eyes of their commander. This edition, also in the Musée de Malmaison,
includes a watercolour by Carle Vernet showing the tome being given to Napoleon by the
artist Berthier; shown here is the preparatory sketch for that painting.

69

The First Consul's suit

Musée national des châteaux
de Malmaison et Bois-Préau
(Fonds Napoléon);
N 259; purchase, 1979 (formerly the
collection of the Imperial family)
Velvet, silk, gold, silver
H. 110
1800

As Napoleon was returning from his second
Italian campaign in 1800 he stopped in
Lyon where the city council presented him
with this richly embroidered suit as evidence
of their city's traditional crafts, which had
suffered as a result of the Revolution. The
First Consul's visit was an opportunity to
impress him and to remind him of the
importance to their city of the traditional
trade in luxury items. Bonaparte wore this
suit for the *Te Deum* sung at Notre-Dame on
April 18, 1802 to celebrate the Concordat and
for the signing ceremony also. It should not
be confused with another red velvet robe
worn in official portraits of the First Consul
painted by Greuze, Gros and Ingres. Napoleon
took this one with him to St. Helena, and in
1818 gave it to Grand Marshal Bertrand's
daughter so she could make a dress from it;
fortunately, she decided to keep it, and later
gave it to Prince Victor Napoleon.

71

First Consul's letter-case

Musée national des châteaux
de Malmaison et Bois-Préau;
MM 40–47–6901;
Gift of M. Barbet, 1930
Morocco leather, silk, gilded brass
L. 48; W. 35
1800–1804

This green-Morocco letter-case stamped
with the First Consul's name was probably
used to carry papers destined for his eyes
only; it has only one pocket inside, whereas
couriers' letter-cases usually had several
compartments, being used to carry papers
from more than one administrative
department.

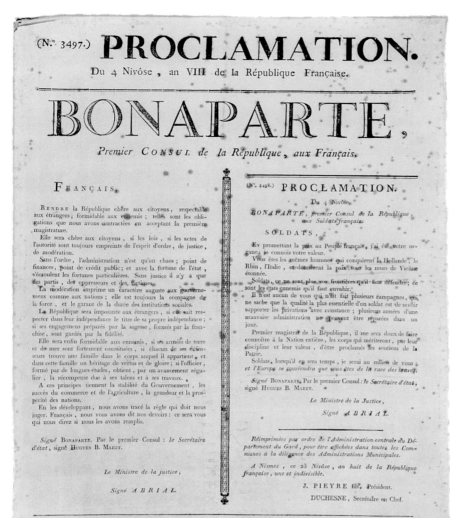

Proclamation of the 4 Nivôse year VIII of Bonaparte First Consul to the French (December 25, 1799)

Poster printed "At Nismes, at the sign of the Veuve Belle, Printers to the Department of the Gard, Place du Château, n° 32"
Musée national des châteaux de Malmaison et Bois-Préau;
MM 40–47–3409;
Gift of Émile Brouwet
Paper
H. 51; W. 39
1799

Once established as the head of the highest court in the land, Bonaparte issued numerous pacifying announcements such as this double proclamation dated December 25, 1799; the lefthand column of the poster is addressed to the French people: "To make the Republic dear to her Citizens, respected by foreigners, formidable to her enemies"; he then speaks to the soldiers, promising them that "When the time comes, I shall be in your midst; and Europe will remember that you come from the race of fighters." In Paris and the big cities people were jubilant at the announcement of the coup d'état, and although the reaction in the provinces was less effusive, no real resistance was seen.

70

Nicolas-Nöel Boutet (1761–1833), director of the munitions factory at Versailles

First Consul's sabre

Paris, Musée de l'Armée; inv. Ca 2100–12274; purchase 1955
Steel, ebony
W. 82 (blade); 96 (without scabbard)
About 1802

The Versailles weapons factory had been set up in the former great hall of the château. It produced the most expensive weapons created during the Consulate and the Empire, especially luxury items and those presented as gifts to leading figures of the régime. This sabre, inscribed on the back of the blade with the inscription "To the 1st Consul", is particularly rich in decoration, much of Egyptian inspiration. This type of sabre was sometimes called a "mourning sabre" because of the dark colour of the blued-steel blade.

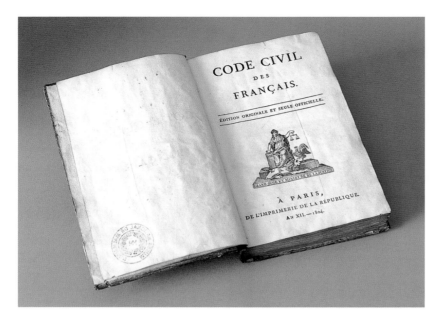

73

Civil Code of the French, Original and Only Official Edition, Paris, year XII 1804

Musée national des châteaux
de Malmaison et Bois-Préau;
MM 4656 (library inventory);
gift of M. Jean Ricard, 1994
Calf, paper
H. 19.5; W. 13
1804

The French Civil Code, promulgated in 1804, was to take the title of Napoleonic Code in 1807. Although the First Consul attended scarcely more than half of the Commission's sessions, the text would never have been published so quickly without his determination; the entire task was completed between 1800 and 1804. The Code is divided into three volumes, the first devoted to persons, the second to possessions and the various exchanges of property, and the third to the different means of acquiring property.

This simply-bound copy is one of the first, original printing, published in 1804.

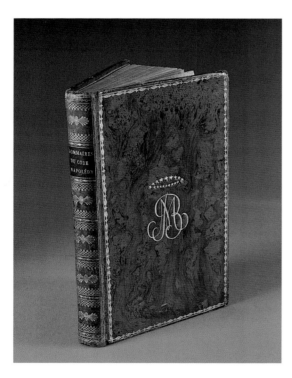

74

Summaries of the 2281 articles that make up the Napoleonic Code. By two former magistrates, Paris, 1810

Musée national des châteaux de Malmaison et Bois-Préau;
MM 40–47–9878
Marbled calf, paper
H. 21; W. 13
1810

To facilitate the finding of a required passage in the many articles of the Napoleonic Code, the two magistrates created a sort of index for the use of readers.

75

Malcom Cameron,
printer to the Queen

Civil Code of Lower Canada, 1866

Montreal, The Stewart Museum at the Fort,
Île Sainte-Hélène; C340.56/Q3c/1866
Paper, leather
H. 14.3; W. 7
Ottawa, Canada; 1866

When Lower Canada was conquered by the English in 1760, civil life in Canada was still ruled by the Coutume de Paris. However, English law applied between 1763 and 1774, when the Quebec Act reinstated the Coutume. Finally the French Civil Code, called the Napoleonic Code after 1807, was used as a basis for the Civil Code of Lower Canada, which came into force on August 1, 1866. In French Canada in the late-19th century the Civil Code of the province of Quebec was still commonly called the Napoleonic Code.
G.V.

77

Pierre-Joseph-Simon Tiolier
(1763–1819)

Forty-franc piece

Musée national des châteaux de Malmaison et Bois-Préau;
MM 40–47–8627;
Gift of Gaston Gérardot de Sermoise
Gold
D. 2,5
1803

78

Jean-Pierre Droz
(1746–1823)
and Pierre-Joseph-Simon Tiolier
(1763–1819)

Twenty-franc piece

Musée national des châteaux de Malmaison et Bois-Préau;
MM 40–47–8628;
Gift of Gaston Gérardot de Sermoise
Gold
D. 2
1806

79

Pierre-Joseph-Simon Tiolier
(1763–1819)

Five-franc piece

Musée national des châteaux de Malmaison et Bois-Préau;
MM 40–47–5451;
Gift of Gaston Gérardot de Sermoise
Silver
D. 3.7
Year XI (1803)

The law of the 17 Germinal year XI (March 28, 1803) called
for the minting of gold forty- and twenty-franc pieces,
other coins being made of silver. This law, the result
of which was the Germinal franc, remained the basis of
the French monetary system until 1928. Each coin bears
on the obverse the First Consul's profile with the words
"Bonaparte First Consul" and "French Republic" followed
by the date of striking. The decree of June 26, 1804
changed the title "Napoleon Emperor", but it was not
until January 1, 1809 that "French Republic" was replaced
by the rather more logical " French Empire". An echo
of the old order is seen in the words around the edge
"God preserve France".

The incomparable engraver-machinist Jean-Pierre Droz
was curator of stamps and dies for coins and medals
from 1803 and 1817; Tiolier, appointed engraver-general
of the Mint in 1803, designed most of the dies for
Napoleonic coins.

81

Nicolas-Noël Boutet (1761–1833),
director of the munitions factory at Versailles

Ceremonial rifle; on the butt a silver shield engraved:
"The First Consul to citizen Rat, fusilier in the 18th regiment of the line, presently unfit for service, in recognition of his distinguished service in the Syrian campaign"

Musée national des châteaux de Malmaison et Bois-Préau;
MMD 3/9 (from the Musée national de la Légion d'honneur et des Ordres de Chevalerie, 1959)
Wood, silver
L. 135; W. 14
About 1800

80

Imprimerie bibliographique,
Obré and Rondonneau, publisher

Code of Civil Procedure, collected edition from the minutes of the State Council.

Montreal, Bibliothèque nationale du Québec;
(general book collection)
346.74/C648R/1806
Paper, leather
H. 13; W. 7
Paris; [1806]

It took much longer to write the Civil Code of Lower Canada than it did the French Civil Code, which was created under the aegis of First Consul Napoleon Bonaparte. In the Bill for the Codification of a Civil Code for Lower Canada of June 10, 1857 legislators decree that "the said codes shall be written according to the same general plan and shall contain, in so far as may be properly be done, the same quantity of details on each subject as the French codes known as the civil code, the code of commerce and the code of civil precedure." (20 V c. 43, §. 7 c).

The instigator was Georges-Étienne Cartier, the Attorney-General of Lower Canada who was to become a Father of Canadian Confederation. The Civil Code of Lower Canada came into force on August 1st, 1866, nine years after the Bill of Codification of 1857.
G.V.

82

Attributed to Nicolas-Noël Boutet (1761–1833),
director of the munitions factory at Versailles

Ceremonial sabre; inscription engraved on the chape of the scabbard *"The First Consul to citizen Soulès, Brigadier-General commanding the infantry of the Consuls' Guard"*

Paris, Musée de l'Armée; inv. Cc 46

In the name of the principle of Equality the Convention had suppressed all the ancient royal orders of chivalry such as the Orders of the Holy Spirit, of St. Michael and St. Louis, but it soon became necessary to find a way of recognising military feats. The Directory accordingly instituted a system of awarding arms of honour awarded to outstanding soldiers. The arm could be a musket, a rifle, a carbine, a trumpet, a grenade, a set of drumsticks, even a marine's hatchet. Most were awarded during the second Italian campaign, especially after the battle of Marengo. This gun was presented after the Syrian campaign to Fusilier François Rat, a wounded lieutenant who could not sign his name; the sabre went to Jérôme Soulès (1760-1833), who had been promoted brigadier-general of the infantry of the Consular Guard on December 6. 1801; he would later be made a general and Count of the Empire by Napoleon.

Nomination and oath of Jean-Nicolas Seroux, Baron du Fay (1742–1822) General of artillery, as a member of the Legion of Honour
Musée national des châteaux
de Malmaison et Bois-Préau; unnumbered
Paper
Nomination: H. 32.2; W. 21.6.
Oath: H. 17.7; W. 20.3
1803

Before the first diplomas were issued under the Restoration, a simple letter from the Grand Chancellor of the Legion of Honour informed the recipient of his nomination to the order. It included a printed form which the new legionnaire had to sign after taking his oath before the president of the tribunal nearest to the place where he had received the letter.

This form, returned to the Grand Chancellery, was worded as follows during the Consulate: "I swear on my honour to devote myself to the service of the Republic; to the preservation of its territory in its integrity; to the defense of its Government, its laws and the lands it holds sacred; to fight, by all means authorised by justice, reason and law, any attempt to restore the feudal regime or to reproduce the titles and ranks pertaining to it; and to work with all my strength to uphold Liberty and Equality."

83

Officer's cross of the Legion of Honour (1st type)

*Musée national des châteaux
de Malmaison et Bois-Préau; MMD 3/5;
(from the Musée national de la Légion
d'honneur et des Ordres de Chevalerie, 1959)
Gold, enamel, silk
H. 4.2; W. 3.7
1804*

It was during a meeting at Malmaison in May 1802 that Bonaparte first formulated the idea of creating an award both civil and military to replace the arms of honour. A decree was composed, not without difficulty as the old monarchical orders had been abolished only ten years earlier. The bill instituting the Legion of Honour was finally voted in by the legislative assembly on May 19, 1802; even as today, the order was intended to reward civil and military merit. Although the first convocation on September 24, 1803 inducted only the 2,000 holders of arms of honour, two splendid ceremonies the following year marked the real birth of the order; the first at the Invalides on July 14, 1804 and the second at Boulogne on August 16, 1804.

There were four types of decoration during the Empire, each slightly different from the others. The design seems to have been the work of David himself. The first type, going back to 1804, does not have the ram's crown; all the other types carry the red taffeta ribbon. The gold decorations, such as this one, were reserved for commanding and senior officers and officers.

Knight's Cross of the Legion of Honour (2nd type)

*Musée national des châteaux
de Malmaison et Bois-Préau;
MMD 3/6;
(from the Musée national de la Légion
d'honneur et des Ordres de Chevalerie, 1959)
Silver, enamel, silk
H. 6.3; W. 3.7
1806*

The second type, designed in 1806, bears a ram-crown with twelve palmettes that is seen on all later examples. This one in silver was the medal reserved for legionnaires.

Knight's Cross of the Legion of Honour (3rd type)

*Musée national des châteaux
de Malmaison et Bois-Préau;
MM 40–47–4728;
Git of Madame de Visme de Wegmann, 1931
Silver, enamel, silk
H. 6.3; W. 3.7
About 1808*

The third type was created in 1808; it differs only slightly from the others.

Knight's Cross of the Legion of Honour (4th type)

*Musée national des châteaux
de Malmaison et Bois-Préau;
MMD 3/8;
(from the Musée national de la Légion
d'honneur et des Ordres de Chevalerie, 1959)
Silver, enamel, silk
H. 6.5; W. 3.7
Late First Empire*

The fourth type was created about 1813 with the single addition of balls on the ends of the branches so as not to tear the fabric of the garment worn with the order.

88

Martin-Guillaume Biennais
(1764–1843)

Collar of Marshal Berthier's Legion of Honour

*Paris, Musée national de la Légion
d'honneur des Ordres de Chevalerie;
inv. 08161
Gold, enamel
H. 40; D. 51 (without cross)
First Empire*

The collar, based on orders of the old regime, was given to a very limited number of people: in addition to the Emperor himself we know of only fourteen recipients, most of them members of the Imperial family. The collar is formed of medallions bearing the numbers of the cohorts linked by eagles grasping lightning bolts. Louis-Alexandre Berthier (1753-1815), ruling Prince of Neuchâtel and Prince of Wagram, was the only Marshal to receive it, having been made Grand Eagle and chief of the 1st cohort of the Legion of Honour in February 1805. The sixteen cohorts were spread throughout the Empire and formed the regional administration of the order; they generally set up their centres in stately homes, archbishops' palaces and abbeys.

1ˢᵗ type   2ⁿᵈ type   3ʳᵈ type   4ᵗʰ type

DISTRIBUTION DE L'ÉTOILE DE LA LÉGION D'HONNEUR.   A L'ARMÉE DES CÔTES DE L'OCÉAN, LE 16 AOÛT 1804.

Dédiée par Ph. Aug. Hennequin   *aux membres de la légion D'honneur*

90

After Philippe-Augustin Hennequin (1763–1833)

Distribution of the Star of the Legion of Honour to the Army of the Ocean Coasts, August 16, 1804. Dedicated by Ph. Aug. Hennequin to the members of the Legion of Honour. Engraved by Hennequin from his painting. Sold at Liège, rue des Carmes, no. 297

Montreal, The Stewart Museum at the Fort, Île Sainte-Hélène; inv. 1970.1183
H. 53; W. 79.5
Liège, Belgium; 1813

This engraving, presented at the Salon de la Société libre d'émulation of Liège in 1813, is a version (with the foreground figures differently disposed) of the painting commissioned from Hennequin in 1804, which he exhibited at the Salon of 1806 (now in the museum of Versailles). Hennequin, the only artist admitted to the ceremony, tells in his memoirs of his journey with Denon: "We had in the carriage the fifteen hundred crosses to be given to the army which, by divisions of fiteen to twenty thousand men, brought the reunion to almost seventy thousand men [...] The Emperor arrived at one o'clock; it was misty weather; the groups on the dunes sheltered under umbrellas; they began to disperse to seek the shelter of the town or the tents set up on the high ground. Napoleon had barely taken his seat on the bronze chair when the sky cleared and the clouds broke up, letting though a beam of sunlight that lit up the trophy in front of the Emperor and showed the flags of all the nations conquered by the armies of France. I was a witness of all that happened on that memorable day and I drew all the details with the greatest precision."

91

Claude Bouvet
(about 1755–1814)

Napoleon I giving out the Legion of Honour

Musée national des châteaux
de Malmaison et Bois-Préau;
MDO 222;
Osiris Bequest, 1912
Cast iron
H. 82; W. 53
1814

On occasion, when he wanted to
single out a recipient for special
honour, Napoleon would present him
with a Legion of Honour he himself
was wearing for the occasion, which
the honoree believed to be the Emperor's
own; he did the same with occasional
gifts of a watch or snuffbox bearing
his initials. Napoleon is seen here
standing bareheaded and in uniform
holding in his right hand a parchment
and a cross of the Legion of Honour.
A coloured plaster version of this statue
is in the musée napoléonien of the
Ile d'Aix (M. GA 38).

Convention entre la République Française et les États-unis d'Amérique, Signée à Mortefontaine le onze Vendémiaire, l'An 9 3 Octobre 1800.

92

Baublé the younger, after Joseph S.W.E. Bach-Desfontaine

Agreement between the French Republic and the United States of America signed at Mortefontaine on the 11 Vendemiaire year IV

Blérancourt, Musée national de la coopération franco-américaine; inv. MNB CFA c 193
Coloured engraving
H. 49; W. 72
18th century

Joseph Bonaparte, ordered by his brother to re-establish harmony between France and the United States, decided to celebrate the agreement between the French and American dignitaries by a grand party given on October 3, 1800 at his estate of Mortefontaine near Paris. Among the 180 guests were the three Consuls, the Ministers of the Republic and Americans residing in Paris, not to mention La Fayette and La Rochefoucauld-Liancourt, formerly resident in America. During the party Napoleon gave a toast "to the Spirits of the Frenchmen and Americans killed on the battelfield for the cause of Independence of the New World." Joseph immediately commissioned from Francesco Piranesi, one of the sons of the great Piranesi, this colour engraving which he had printed in a limited edition and sold at 40 francs each.

Bill of the Louisiana Purchase

Paris, Ministry of Foreign Affairs
Paper, wax
H. 36; W. 24
1803

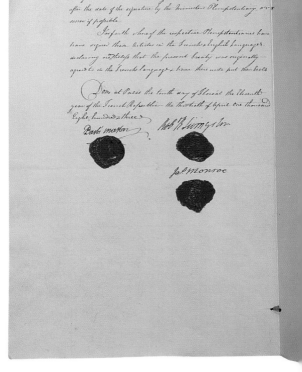

Following the Treaty of Paris in 1763, France had been obliged to cede
Louisiana to Spain. In 1800 after the victory of Marengo that opened
the gates of Italy to him, Bonaparte negotiated with the Spanish
Bourbon monarchy to have Louisiana restored to France in return
for the creation of the kingdom of Etruria, given to the Duke of Parma
who had married the daughter of the Spanish monarchs. This
exchange was the subject of a secret treaty signed at San Idelfonso
on October 1, 1800. A year later on October 2, 1801 the ratification
of this treaty was signed in the council chamber at Malmaison and
Louisiana was ceded to France. Bonaparte initially envisaged a military
occupation of the colony, but faced with the concern expressed by
the American government and the risk of renewed conflict with
England, he decided to sell Louisiana for 60 million francs and an
additional 20 million of indemnities, a total of 15 million dollars.
The official bill was signed in Paris on April 30, 1803 by Barbé-Marbois,
Minister of the Treasury, and by President Jefferson's two envoys,
Robert Livingston and James Monroe, who was to become fifth
president of the United States. By this purchase the United States
doubled the extent of their territory, as the former colony of Louisiana
was equivalent to the present states of Missouri, Arkansas, Minnesota,
Kansas, Nebraska, Colorado, the two Dakotas, Montana, Wyoming and
Oklahoma. Napoleon thus made the United States one of the largest
countries in the world and opened the way to the West.

94

Bouch

Thomas Jefferson

Musée national des châteaux de Malmaison et Bois-Préau; MM 58–7–2;
Gift of Baroness Napoleon Gourgaud (née Eva Gebhard) 1958.
Charcoal with chalk highlights on paper; signed and dated, lower left:
"Bouch f[ecit] l'an 9"
H. 25; W. 20
1801

Thomas Jefferson (1743-1826) was a wealthy Virginia planter who was
asked to compose the Declaration of Independence in 1776. He represented the United States at the court of France from 1784 to 1789, was
elected President of the United States in 1801, and despite his doubts
about the validity of the acquisition, agreed to the Louisiana Purchase
in 1803. Reelected in 1804, Jefferson remained president until 1809.

A reproduction of the print of the portrait of Jefferson painted by
Rembrandt Peale in 1800 (now in the Peabody Institute, Baltimore),
this drawing was probably a gift from the President's representatives on
the occasion of the Louisiana Purchase. It remained in the Malmaison
collection until the sale of 1829, when it was bought by General
Gourgaud, a companion of the Emperor on St. Helena; it remained in
his family until returned to Malmaison in 1958.

95

Pierre-Joseph-Célestin François (1759–1851)

Allegory of the Concordat

Musée national des châteaux de Malmaison et Bois-Préau; MM 40–47–6886;
Gift of Baroness d'Alexandry d'Orengiani, 1924
H. 103; W. 135
1802

Religious peace was part of Bonaparte's plan, as it also meant civil peace. He recognised that the people needed religion, and swiftly entered into negotiations with the new Pope Pius VII. The Concordat, signed in Paris on July 15, 1801 at midnight, provided for the resignation of the constitutional clergy and the recognition of the sales of ecclesiastical property by the Revolution. It was not published in Rome until April 18, 1802 and it was not easy to apply in a France still marked by revolutionary anticlericalism. Only the Pope's religious zeal and Bonaparte's political will enabled the treaty to remain in force until 1905.

The event was celebrated in the form of a competition in painting, medal-casting, sculpture and architecture; entries had to be submitted before December 6, 1802. Paintings had to be represented by a 13-square-metre sketch like this one, although François' work was not selected by the jury. The symbolic imagery was probably not to Bonaparte's liking.

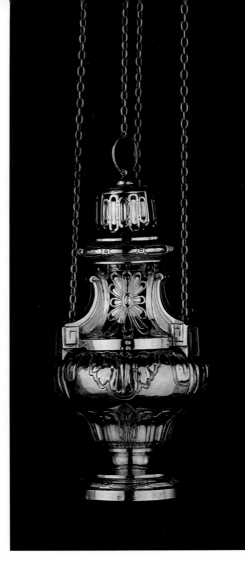

96

Anonymous

Censer

Montreal, collection of the Honourable Serge Joyal,
Senator, P. C., C. O.
Silver, brass (chain); inscription "Given to
the Church of [Mive] in 1818 by mʳ Lancin of Paris.";
bears the hallmark Paris 1809–1819
H. 26.7
Paris, France; between 1809 and 1819

The decoration here is splendid, with a base
ornamented with ova and pearls together with
boss beading and lanceolate forms, acanthus
leaves and scrolls in thick rich silver; the hole
under the base held a nut and screw.
R.D.

97

Anonymous (unidentified provincial
master-goldsmith)

Sanctuary lamp

Montreal, collection of the Honourable Serge Joyal,
Senator, P. C., C. O.
Silver, metal; bears the hallmarks
of the departements 1809–1819 and of
an unidentified master-goldsmith (S.)
H. 26.7 (lamp without chain)
France; between 1809 and 1819

The engraving is embossed with chasing,
and the ornamentation of large palms,
leaves and rosettes. The pommel of the lamp
stand has undergone significant repair,
leaving a separation line clearly visible.
R.D.

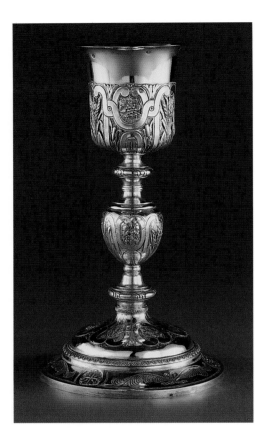

98

Edme Gelez, active in Paris between 1812 and 1822

Chalice

Montréal, collection of the Honourable Serge Joyal, Senator, P. C., C. O.
Silver, interior of vessel gilt; bears the hallmarks of Paris
1809–1819 and of the master-goldsmith Gelez
H. 29.5
Paris, France; between 1812/1813 and 1819

This is a magificent piece in thick metal. The chalice is
decorated with vine leaves and reeds, the base with palms.
R.D.

99

Anonymous (unidentified provincial
master-goldsmith)

Ciborium

Montreal, collection of the Honourable Serge Joyal,
Senator, P. C., C. O.
Silver, interior of vessel and lid gilt; bears
the hallmarks of the departements 1798–1809
and of an unidentified master-goldsmith (A.L.)
H. 25.8
France; between 1798 and 1809

Here the simple decoration consists
of chasing, interlacing, reeds and vines,
with lanceolate motifs around the lid.
The bottom of the cup is thin and flat.
R.D.

100

Anonymous (unidentified provincial master-goldsmith)

Monstrance

Montreal, collection of the Honourable Serge Joyal, Senator, P. C., C. O.
Silver; bears the hallmarks of the departments 1798–1809 and of an unidentified master-goldsmith (R S)
H. 51
France; between 1798 and 1809

The decoration is divided into three parts: on the base chasing composed of garlands of rosettes, a frieze of laurel leaves, the Tables of the Law, vineleaves, wheat and the triangle of Jehovah; on the knot, lanceolate forms and water lily leaves; clouds and cherubim on the sunburst.
R.D.

101

Anonymous (unidentified Parisian master-goldsmith)

Small ciborium and vessels for holy oils

Montreal, collection of the Honourable Serge Joyal, Senator, P. C., C. O.
Silver, interior of cup and lid gilt; bears the hallmarks of 1789 and of repair work in the perios 1798–1809 and 1819–1838, together with that of an unidentified master-goldsmith (NTC)
H. 12.1
Paris, France; 1789

A superb example of the complexity of hallmarks during the Revolutionary period, and also of the vicissitudes of precious metalwork at the time. Some hallmarks were not published. This specimen happily escaped being melted down, but has undoubtedly been repaired several times. It ia a multi-purpose vessel, appropriate to Revolutionary period but in spirit completely of the old order. It is simple, undecorated, with just a slight rounded curve; the stem holds a small spatula for the holy oils.
R.D.

IV

1804-1815

IV

Emperor Napoleon I

102

Jean-Baptiste-Claude-<u>Eugène</u> Guillaume
(1822–1905)

Napoleon I in 1806

Musée national des châteaux
de Malmaison et Bois-Préau;
MM 40–47–6845;
Gift of Madame Henri Lefuel,
descendent of the sculptor
Plaster
H. 80; W. 65
Second Empire

This bust is one of a series of six
sculpted portraits of Napoleon at
different stages of his life.

On May 18, 1804 the government of the Republic was handed over to Napoleon Bonaparte, who took the title Emperor of the French.

There was a rush to form part of a court around the Emperor and Empress. Napoleon wanted his court to be sumptuous and provided lavishly for every member of his family, as court life entailed expenditure on luxuries that supported industry and encouraged the arts. He set up house in the various royal palaces, which he found empty, and within a few years restored them to their former glories of furniture and décor. The culmination of all this extravagance was the unprecedented pomp of Napoleon's Anointing and Coronation in Notre-Dame-de-Paris on December 2, 1804. The Pope, resigned to it, was asked to come to Paris for the new ruler's ceremonies of investiture. Some months later, on May 26, 1805 in Milan, Napoleon, now King of Italy, placed on his own head the iron crown of the Lombard kings.

As Emperor he proceeded to revive the old royal customs, setting up his House and that of the Empress in the same style as their predecessors King Louis XVI and Marie-Antoinette. The etiquette of the imperial palace governed every moment of their lives, but both adapted to it admirably, Josephine assuming her new role with universally recognised grace and tact. Away from his public performance, Napoleon made himself at home with his familiar patterns and work habits. Grandeur he sought above all, for to him everything that was imposing was beautiful. He influenced the arts of his time by commissioning works glorifying his deeds and by beautifying Paris; in the few years of his reign he was only able to begin his design for an imperial capital by building the arch on the Place du Carrousel, the Vendôme column, the Exchange and the arcaded Rue de Rivoli.

109

Studio of François, Baron Gérard
(1779–1839)

**Portrait bust of Napoleon I
in Coronation Robes**

Musée national des châteaux
de Malmaison et Bois-Préau;
MM 40–47–3305;
(from the national porcelain factory
of Sèvres, 1921)
Oil on canvas (oval)
H. 81; L. 65.5
First Empire

This bust from Gérard's studio comes from
the Sèvres factory where it was used as a
model by the artists who were reproducing
the Emperor's portrait on porcelain vases and
cups. It is based on a detail from the large
standing portrait commissioned in 1805
for the Ministry of External Affairs building
(possibly the one now in the Versailles
museum). The work was so successful that
many copies of it were made for Grand
Officers and foreign royalty; some twenty
standing versions have been identified, as
well as innumerable busts. Napoleon wears
here the grand robes of the Anointing,
of which only the tunic, the gold-fringed
sash and the former First Consul's sword
still exist, in the collection of the Musée
de Fontainebleau.

103

The Anointing and Coronation of H.M. the Emperor Napoleon

Musée national des châteaux
de Malmaison et Bois-Préau;
MM 53–3–1;
Gift of Charles Gillet, 1953
Morocco leather, paper
H. 60; W. 47
First Empire

In March 1805 *Le Moniteur* announced the publication of a book describing the Anointing and Coronation ceremonies. A single, unique copy (designed by Isabey, Percier and Fontaine and now in the Musée de Fontainebleau) was intended for the Emperor, and the first printed copies were commissioned later. For some unknown reason we know of only a very few of the latter: this one, bound in London, is signed L. Staggenmeier with the date 1805, which must have been written after the event as at that date none of the plates had yet appeared. Sixteen engravers were commissioned for the task, more as a means of helping artists than of finishing the job more quickly. The book is open at the plate showing the departure from the Tuileries en route to Notre-Dame; the morning of the coronation the cannon fired at eleven o'clock to tell the Parisians that the Emperor and Empress were leaving the palace; the shining gold carriage pulled by eight horses proceeded slowly through the city streets towards the cathedral. The palace of the Tuileries, begun in the 16th century by Catherine de Médicis, stood at the end of the Louvre and had been used as a residence by the Royal family after they left Versailles in 1789; Napoleon moved into the palace in early 1800. It continued to be used as a residence by the 19th-century kings of France until 1870, but in 1871 during the Commune it was burned down, and the ruins cleared away twenty years later.

104

Jacques Lavallée (1745-about 1807),
after Jean-Baptiste Isabey (1767–1855)
and Charles Percier (1764–1838)

The Coronation

Musée national des châteaux de Malmaison et Bois-Préau;
MM 40–47–4347;
Gift of Madame Philippe de Vilmorin, 1926
Colour engraving on paper, taken from the Book of the Coronation
H. 46; W. 58
First Empire

After many royalist conspiracies against the First Consul, countered by the execution of the Duc d'Enghien, a new Constitution was declared on May 18, 1804; article number 1 proclaimed that "The government of the Republic has been entrusted to an Emperor who takes the title of Emperor of the French"; article 2 named the incumbent, Napoleon Bonaparte. Having prevailed upon Pope Pius VII to come and preside over the Anointing and Coronation in Paris, he set the date for December 2, 1804.

The Coronation, different from the Anointing, was the moment for the Pope to place the crown on the new sovereign's head. Rejecting tradition, Napoleon decided to crown himself; taking the gold crown in both hands, he slowly raised it high and then brought it majestically down upon his head. On his own authority he then decided to crown Josephine himself: the Empress, kneeling with bent head, wept as she received from her husband the greatest honour she had ever dreamed of. This was the moment immortalised by the painter David.

Plate: "The Emperor and the Empress leaving *les Tuileries*"

105

Guide to the Personages Appearing in the painting of the Anointing by Jacques-Louis David (1748–1825)

Musée national des châteaux
de Malmaison et Bois-Préau;
MM 58.3.320;
Gift of Princess George of Greece, 1958 (formerly the Demidoff collection, Prince of San Donato, later passed to Roland Bonaparte, father of the donor)
Black-and-white engraving
H. 28; W. 57
Early-19th century

Painted following a personal request from the Emperor about September 1804, the enormous canvas (H. 629; W. 979) was completed by November 1807 and retouched at Napoleon's order in January 1808 (it is now in the Louvre Museum; a copy in oils painted between 1808 and 1822 is in the Musée de Versailles).

108

Louis-Pierre Deseine (1749–1822)

Pope Pius VII

Musée national des châteaux
de Malmaison et Bois-Préau;
MM 40–47–6028;
Gift of M. Le Chatelier, 1923
Platinised plaster, terracotta; signed and
dated on the back: "made at Paris, from life,
in 1805 by de Seine".
H. 47; L. 35
1805

106

Georges Malbeste (1754–1843)
and Jean-Baptiste-Michel Dupreel
(active between 1787 and 1828),
after Charles Percier (1764–1838)

The Emperor in the Coronation Robes

Musée national des châteaux
de Malmaison et Bois-Préau;
MM 40–47–9570;
Gift of Edward Tuck
Colour engraving on paper, taken from
the Book of the Coronation
H. 56; W. 35.5
First Empire

These are the coronation robes that
appear in most of the official portraits
of Napoleon, of which that by Gérard
is the prototype. Over a long white silk
robe girdled with a gold-fringed sash
(both in the Fontainebleau museum)
he wears the great cloak of purple velvet,
embroidered with golden bees and lined
with ermine,which would be sold at
the Restoration by the canons of Notre-
Dame. Also lost to us are the satin
slippers and white, gold-embroidered
gloves, the cravat and lace shirt-collar,
as is the crown of gold bay leaves.
Napoleon wore the robes only once, for
the ceremony; when he left the Tuileries
to go to Notre-Dame he was wearing
Spanish-style dress of gold-embroidered
purple velvet sparkling with gems.

107

Pierre Audouin (1768–1822),
after Jean-Baptiste Isabey
(1767–1855)
and Charles Percier (1764–1838)

The Empress in the Coronation Robes

Musée national des châteaux
de Malmaison et Bois-Préau;
MM 40–47–9571;
Gift of Edward Tuck
Colour engraving on paper, taken from
the Book of the Coronation
H. 56; L. 35.5
First Empire

Like the Emperor, the Empress wore
day dress before the ceremony at Notre-
Dame and then at the Archbishop's
palace donned the grand robes seen in
the official portrait by Gérard (see 110).
These consisted of the long purple
velvet cloak sewn with gold bees and
lined with ermine, the long-sleeved
gown of silver brocade, the hem adorned
with gold fringes and a diamond-
studded bodice. Most of these garments
disappeared after the Restoration.

Barnabé Chiaramonti (1742-1823) was
elected Pope in 1800, shortly after
the seizure of power by Bonaparte,
whose iron fist dominated his entire
papacy. Without ever compromising
on religious matters, he signed
the Concordat of 1801, thus granting
official existence to the Church in France.
Although he went to Paris in 1804 to
crown Napoleon, he always opposed
the Emperor's expansionist designs.
Their struggle was to end with
Napoleon's annexation of the Papal
States to the French Empire followed by
the Pope's captivity from 1809 to 1814.
His papacy ended, however, in less
hectic circumstances, and Pius VII was
magnanimous enough to welcome
the exiled Bonapartes to his States and
later to ask the allied powers to mitigate
the harshness of Napoleon's captivity.

As the statement on the bust claims,
this work was executed from life.
The artist, who held a privileged
position at Notre-Dame, in fact was
granted several sittings by the Pope;
he kept this model in his studio.

110

Studio of François, Baron Gérard
(1779–1839)

Portrait bust of the Empress Josephine in the Anointing Robes
Musée national des châteaux de Malmaison et Bois-Préau;
MM 40–47–3304;
(from the national porcelain factory of Sèvres, 1921)
Oil on canvas (oval)
H. 81; L. 65.5
First Empire

Like the portrait of the Emperor, this painting was used by artists
at the Sèvres factory. It is a version of the bust in the official portrait
of the Empress commissioned from Gérard in 1807 and shown at
the Salon of 1808. Gérard made several versions of it; we know of
five, one of them in the Fontainebleau museum. The Empress wears
here some of the Anointing robes including the purple velvet cloak.

111

Possibly Martin-Guillaume Biennais (1764–1843)

Pair of cross-legged stools
Musée national des châteaux de Malmaison et Bois-Préau;
MM 65–3–15 and 16;
Gift of Baronness Gourgaud (née Eva Gebhard) 1965
Mahogany, gilded bronze
H. 64; W. 115; L. 53
First Empire

This type of stool, of which several are known, is traditionally held to have been reserved
for Marshals. A recently discovered archival document seems to corroborate this hypothesis;
in a letter to Prince Eugène dated October 17, 1821 his steward Baron Darnay writes after
visiting Biennais's studio: "I have seen cross-legged stools made to seat the Marshals of
France around the Throne (twelve were ordered, but only three made); the X is composed
of sabres, it is of great size and beauty for a library or study. Each stool should cost
1,800 F. If Your Highness has orders, I will carry them out." Eugène did not
purchase them.

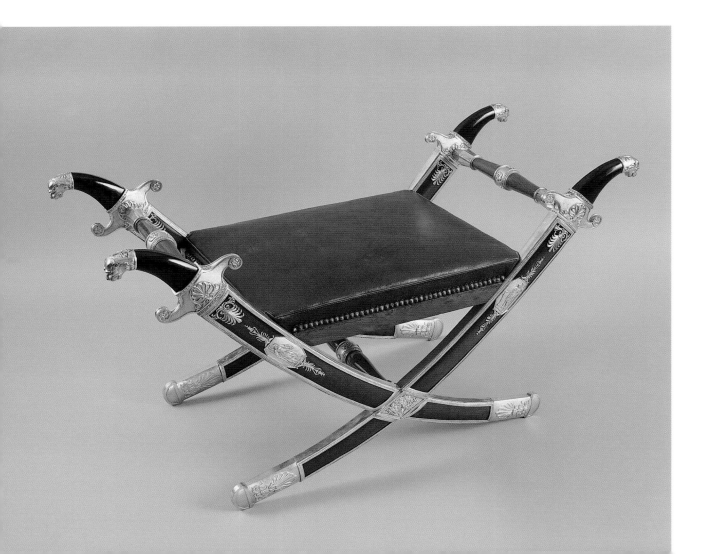

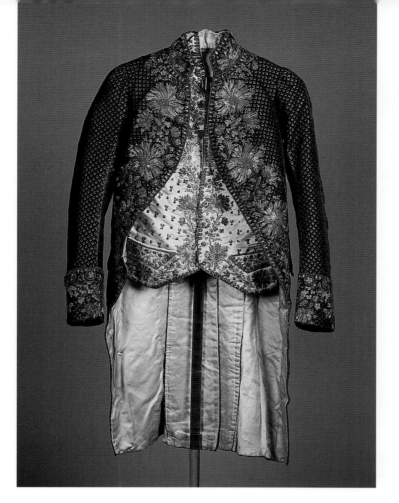

112

Waistcoat and jacket of a man's suit in the French style

Montreal, The Stewart Museum at the Fort, Île Sainte-Hélène; inv. 1982.72
Black and brown velvet embroidered with silk thread and silver
France, about 1800

113

Waistcoat and jacket of a suit in the French style

Montreal, The Stewart Museum at the Fort, Île Sainte-Hélène; inv. 1982.33
Brown silk and raw silk embroidered with silk thread
France, about 1800

Comb belonging to Pauline Borghèse
Collection of Élaine Bédard - Alexandre
de Bothuri Báthory
Gold, cameos
H. 14; W. 21

Like all the princesses of the
Imperial family, Pauline received
from her brother numerous jewels,
some of which are mentioned in
the archives; thus we know that
Napoleon bought for her from the
jeweller Devoix a dazzling head-
dress made of 194 turquoises and
316 carats of diamond brilliants
at a total cost of 74,988 F. The
princess had a special affection
for mounted cameos such as
the head-dress of cameos and
diamonds seen in her portrait
painted by Robert Lefèvre. The comb
in the painting is almost identical
to this one, with only slight differ-
ences in the profiles. This sort of
comb was worn high on the head
above the tiara, which rested on
the brow.

**Set of jewellery once belonging
to Queen Hortense**
Musée national des châteaux
de Malmaison et Bois-Préau;
MM 40–47–6926;
Gift of Comte Raoul Desmazières-
Marchand, 1924 (grandson
of the Emperor's valet on St. Helena,
Louis Marchand)
Coral, pearls, gold, silver
H. 2.5; W. 17
First Empire

This set, made up of a bracelet, four
brooches and four pins was given by
Queen Hortense to Madame Marchand,
née Mathilde Brayer (1805-1881),
daughter of the General Comte Brayer,
who in 1823 married the former first
valet (or manservant) to the Emperor
at St. Helena, Louis-Joseph-Narcisse
Marchand (1791-1876).

**Mourning diadem
of Queen Hortense**

Musée national des châteaux
de Malmaison et Bois-Préau;
MM 40–47–7169;
Gift of Madame Donzel, 1939
Gilded bronze, jet
H. 7; W. 19; L. 16.
First Empire or Restoration

Jet, a sort of shiny-black lignite,
was used in the early-19th century
to make mourning jewellery; it was
later replaced by coloured glass.
This diadem or tiara, the sole
remaining piece of a set, was
worn by Queen Hortense who
later gave it to her lady-in-waiting
Valérie Masuyer (1798-1878), the
Empress Joséphine's goddaughter.
It passed thereafter to her great-
niece Madame Donzel, who
donated it to the Musée de
Malmaison in 1939.

**Crucifix and pair of earrings
possibly belonging to Queen
Caroline Murat**

Musée national des châteaux
de Malmaison et Bois-Préau;
MM 63–4–6;
Gift of Mrs Louise Schneider, 1962
(from her relative Louis Mailliard,
executor of King
Joseph's will)
Moonstones, chalcedony, gold
Crucifix: H. 9; W. 4.5
Earrings: W. 2.5; D. 1.5
First Empire

Chalcedony is a variety of agate
characterised by a more or less
pronounced milky opalescence.
Queen Caroline Murat, the
probable owner of the crucifix
and earrings, may have given them
to her niece Charlotte Bonaparte
(1802-1839), daughter of King
Joseph, who had married her first
cousin Prince Napoleon Louis
Bonaparte (1804-1831), son of King
Louis and Queen Hortense; he was
the elder brother of the future
Napoléon III.

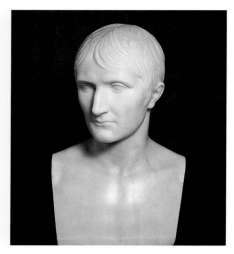

122

Carrara workshops, probably
after François-Nicolas Delaistre
(1746–1832)

**Joseph Bonaparte, King of Naples,
then of Spain**

Ajaccio, Musée national de la maison
Bonaparte; (Fonds Napoléon); N 38;
Gift of T.I.H. Prince and Princess
Napoleon Bonaparte, 1979 (formerly
the Princess of Moskowa, + 1949,
descendant of both Joseph and Lucien)
Marble
H. 48
First Empire

Joseph Bonaparte was the eldest
of Charles and Letizia's children. He was
born in Corte in 1768 and in 1794 married
Julie Clary, the daughter of a wealthy
Marseilles merchant. Involved as he was
in his brother's rise to power, he kept
for himself the diplomatic business,
negotiating with the United States
(the Mortefontaine treaty), Austria and
England. He was already a senator
and a Grand Officer of the Legion of
Honour when in 1806 the Emperor
offered him the kingdom of Naples; he
accepted, and in 1808 swapped it for the
throne of Spain. After the French defeat
he was obliged to leave Madrid; in 1814
Napoleon appointed him lieutenant-
general with the mission of defending
Paris. Joseph had to abandon the capital
and retired to Switzerland; during
the Hundred Days he held the chair
of the Council of Ministers while the
Emperor was away. After Waterloo
he fled to the United States and set up
house in Point Breeze, near Philadelphia.
Joseph died in Florence in 1844.

123

Possibly by Pietro Marchetti
(+ 1846), probably by
Antonio Canova (1757–1822)

Lucien Bonaparte, Prince of Canino

Ajaccio, musée national de la maison
Bonaparte; (Fonds Napoléon); N 39;
Gift of T.I.H. Prince and Princess
Napoléon Bonaparte, 1979 (formerly
the Princess of Moskowa, +1949,
descendant of both Joseph and Lucien)
Marble
H. 48
First Empire

The Bonapartes' third son was born
in Ajaccio in 1775. After fighting for
the Jacobin cause during the Revolution,
Lucien gradually became prominent,
and in 1799 was appointed chairman
of the Five Hundred, one of the two
assemblies then governing France.
He played a vital role in the coup d'état
of the 18 Brumaire which brought his
brother to power, and was made
Minister of the Interior and later
ambassador to Madrid. Shortly after
the death of his first wife, Lucien
decided to marry Alexandrine Jacob de
Bleschamp at the very moment when
Napoleon was thinking of marrying him
to the Queen of Etruria. The tiff between
the brothers developed into a real
quarrel, and Lucien fled to Rome, in
the Papal States. In 1810, shortly after
the annexation of Rome by France,
he tried to flee to America but was
captured at sea by the English and
obliged to spend three long years under
house arrest In England. It was not until
1815 that the brothers were reconciled,
and Lucien was made a prince of France.
He would spend the rest of his life in
Italy, dying in Viterbo in 1840.

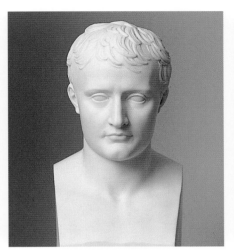

118

Carrara workshops, probably
after Lorenzo Bartolini
(1777–1850)

Élisa Bonaparte

Musée national des châteaux
de Malmaison et Bois-Préau;
MM 40–47–814;
(from Versailles, 1907)
Marble
H. 68
About 1810

The eldest Bonaparte daughter was
born in Ajaccio in 1777. As a child
of noble birth she was admitted to
the École de Saint-Cyr, where she proved
to be a good student. In 1797 at the age
of twenty she married a mediocre
Corsican officer called Félix Bacciochi
(1762-1841). Élisa learned young to
compensate for her unattractiveness by
gratifying her insatiable ambition;
in 1805 she obtained the Principality
of Piombino, in 1806 that of Lucca;
finally, in 1808, she became Grand
Duchess of Tuscany. She settled in
Florence and took her role as sovereign
very seriously as a patron and
protectress of letters and the arts. Élisa
administered her domains with
considerable competence, while her
husband was content to play the roles
of powerless Prince Consort and
consenting cuckold. After the fall
of the Empire Élisa retreated to Italy,
dying in 1820, in her villa near Trieste.

119

Jean-Jacques Oger
(1759–1842),
after Antoine-Denis Chaudet
(1763–1810)

**Bust of Napoleon I
(smaller size)**

Musée national des châteaux
de Malmaison et Bois-Préau;
MM 61–4–1; Purchase, 1961
Bisque, hard paste, Sèvres factory
H. 28.5 (pedestal of red marble and gilded
bronze H. 16; L. 18.5)
1808

Part of the mandate of the Sèvres
factory was to make and sell large
numbers of copies of official portraits
of reigning monarchs. With the advent
of the Empire Napoleon selected for
reproduction the bust Chaudet had
executed during the Consulate; from
1805 it was reproduced in two sizes,
this one being the smaller size. This
bust replaced two models of Napoleon
created in 1798 by the sculptor Boizot.

124

Jean-Jacques Oger
(1759–1842),
after Antoine-Denis Chaudet
(1763–1810)

**Bust of the Empress Joséphine
(smaller size)**

Musée national des châteaux
de Malmaison et Bois-Préau;
MM 61–4–2; Purchase, 1961
Bisque, hard paste, Sèvres factory
H. 30 (pedestal of red marble and gilded
bronze H. 16; L. 18.5)
1808

Chaudet sculpted a bust of Joséphine
to make a pair with that of Napoleon
which the factory was producing in
1808; it was soon replaced by the bust
of the Empress commissioned from
Bosio, which is still in the factory's
catalogue.

The smaller bust of the Emperor sold
at 60 F, while that of the Empress cost
72 F, as the fashioning of the diadem
involved more detailed work. This pair
may well have been one of
the three pairs of smaller busts presented by the Emperor on August 16, 1809
to three members of the Council of
State -- Comte Philippe-Antoine
Merlin de Douai (1754-1838), Comte
Jean-Baptiste Treilhard (1742-1810) and
Comte François Jaubert (1758-1822) --
although we cannot be sure to which
of the three they belonged.

129

Studio of Christophe Blary

Prince Eugène de Beauharnais

Musée national des châteaux
de Malmaison et Bois-Préau;
MM 99–3–1;
Modern moulding after an anonymous
original in marble, dated about
1815–1820; Musée national des
châteaux de Malmaison et Bois-Préau
(Fonds Napoléon); N 3105; dation, 1988;
formerly the collections of the Imperial family
H. 59
Resin
1999

Eugène, born in 1781, was Hortense's
elder brother. As his father Alexandre
de Beauharnais had been guillotined,
his mother's remarriage to young
General Bonaparte provided him with
a readymade military career. He became
aide-de-camp to his father-in-law,
following him in all his campaigns,
and the advent of the Empire made him
a Prince of France and Archchancellor
of State. Appointed Viceroy of Italy he
reigned in Milan between 1805 and 1814
together with his wife Auguste-Amélie,
daughter of the new king of Bavaria
whom he had married in 1806 after
becoming Napoleon's adopted son.
Eugène was exiled to Bavaria after
Waterloo, made Duke of Leuchtenberg
by the King of Bavaria, and died
prematurely in Munich of a stroke.
His children made brilliant marriages,
and his descendants today include the
Kings of Sweden, Norway and Belgium,
the Queens of Denmark and Greece, the
Grand-duchess of Luxembourg and
the Margrave (Marquis) of Baden.

130

François-Joseph Bosio
(1768–1845)

Queen Hortense

Musée national des châteaux
de Malmaison et Bois-Préau;
MM 40–47–6953;
Gift of Mariano de Unzue, 1929
Marble
H. 58
Salon of 1810

Hortense de Beauharnais was
Joséphine's daughter by her first
marriage to the Viscomte Alexandre de
Beauharnais. When she was nineteen in
1802 her mother arranged her marriage
to Napoleon's brother Louis Bonaparte
in the hope of avoiding her own divorce.
Joséphine hoped that any children of
this marriage would be adopted by the
Emperor and thus would inherit the
throne in the absence of the heir she
herself was unable to give Napoleon.
Louis and Hortense became King and
Queen of Holland from 1806 and 1810,
and had three sons, the youngest of
whom would reign from 1852 to 1870
as the Emperor Napoleon III. Despite
the birth of children the marriage was
an unhappy one, and the pair separated.
Hortense was sent into exile after
Waterloo and retired to the small
chateau of Arenenberg in Switzerland,
where she died in 1837.

125

Workshops of Carrara,
after Pierre Cartellier
(1757–1831)

Louis Bonaparte

Boulogne-Billancourt, Bibliothèque
Marmottan; inv. 70–332;
(from one of the palaces of King Jérôme
of Westphalia, near Kassel)
Marble
H. 54
First Empire

Louis Bonaparte was born in Ajaccio
in 1778. He was brought up by his
brother Napoleon, becoming his aide
de camp in Italy and then in Egypt.
Josephine, wishing to strengthen
the links between the Beauharnais and
the Bonapartes, decided in 1802 to marry
him to her own daughter, young
Hortense de Beauharnais. The marriage
was an unhappy one and ended in
separation, despite the birth of three
sons the youngest of whom would
become the Emperor Napoleon III. Louis
was made Grand Constable once the
Empire was established, and
in 1806 King of Holland. There he
sought to defend his peoples against
the Emperor's policies and to evade his
brother's authority by supporting
Holland's interests rather than
maintaining the Continental Blockade.
In desperation he fled to Austria in 1810,
and Holland was immediately annexed
by the French Empire. Louis retired
permanently from politics to devote
himself to literature; he was in Rome
when the Empire fell. He died
in Livorno in 1846.

126

Possibly by Bartolomeo Franzoni,
after the statue by Antonio Canova
(1757–1822) in the Galerie
Borghèse

Pauline Bonaparte

Musée national des châteaux
de Malmaison et Bois-Préau;
MM 40–47–6835;
Gift of Comte Joseph Primoli,
great-grandson of Joseph and Lucien
(formerly the collection of the Empress Eugénie)
Marble
H. 45
First Empire

Pauline was born in Ajaccio in 1780.
Her precocious beauty attracted many
suitors, so in 1797 Napoleon decided
to marry her off young to a brave
soldier, General Victor-Emmanuel
Leclerc (1772–1802). Leclerc died within
five years, of yellow fever contracted
during the doomed expedition to Santo
Domingo. Bonaparte allowed her only
a brief disturbed widowhood before
marrying her in 1803 to Prince Camille
Borghèse (1775-1832), son and heir of
one of the most illustrious families
in Rome. Pauline, a princess by marriage
and ruling Duchess of Guastalla,
separated from her husband in 1806
and thereafter led a life of luxury filled
with numerous love affairs. However,
she remained devoted to her older
brother, whom she followed to the
island of Elba in 1814, and tried unsuccessfully to join him on St. Helena.
She retired to Italy and died in Florence
in 1825.

120

Auguste-Marie Liancé
(1771–1820)
after Antoine-Denis Chaudet
(1763–1810)

Bust of Napoleon I (smaller size)

New York, Malmaison Antiques
Bisque, hard paste, Sèvres factory;
blue-grey marble
H. 45; W. 34
1812

This bust of Napoleon "with crown and
draperies" is from an adaptation made
in early 1811 of the model Chaudet had
sent to Sèvres in the fall of 1804, which
began to be produced in 1805 (see 119).
It was remodelled to make a pair with
the bust of the new Empress. The first
copies of the Emperor's bust were
produced in the smaller size in
April 1811; from that date until the fall
of the Empire nineteen of them were
turned out. This one bears the stamp
of the factory director Alexandre
Brongniart and the date December 31,
1812; the repairer Liancé, who was paid
40 francs, made two in the smaller size
that same month. The finished bust
cost 60 francs for the smaller size,
90 francs with the pedestal, while the
larger one sold for 1,200 francs.

121

Auguste-Marie Liancé
(1771–1820)
after François-Joseph Bosio
(1768–1845)

**Bust of the Empress Marie-Louise
(smaller size)**

New York, Malmaison Antiques
Bisque, hard paste, Sèvres factory;
blue-grey marble
H. 45; W. 34
1812

In December 1810 the first busts
of Marie-Louise after Bosio's model
came out of the factory's kilns; portraits
of the new Imperial couple had to be
made quickly, to be given as presents.
Like that of the Emperor, this bust was
produced in two sizes and sold at
the same prices. This example also
bears the date December 31, 1812 and
Brongniart's stamp. The pair of busts
may be those sold on January 30, 1813
to the Darte brothers, china manufacturers, a firm that held the title
"Manufacturers of porcelain to H(er)
I(mperial) H(ighness) Madame the
Mother of H(is) M(ajesty) the Emperor
and King".

131

Pietro Tenerani
(1789–1869)

The Duc de Reichstadt

Musée national du château
de Fontainebleau (from the Musée
de Malmaison); MM 40–47–8235.
Commissioned by the Comtesse Camerata,
daughter of Élisa Bonaparte who
bequeathed it to the Prince Imperial; the
bust then entered the Empress Eugenie's
collection and was later acquired by the
antiquarian Fabius; purchased in 1945 by
the Musée de Malmaison from M. Fabius.
Marble
H. 73
About 1825–1830

A little more than three months after
his divorce from Josephine Napoleon
married the young Archduchess Marie-
Louise of Austria. On March 20, 1811
the "womb" he had wed produced a son
who was immediately given the title of
King of Rome, after the Empire's second
city. Napoleon, who idolised the child,
saw him for the last time on January 25,
1814; the little king left France at the
age of three and went to live in Vienna
with his grandfather the Emperor of
Austria. As Marie-Louise went to reign
in Parma, he bore the title of Prince of
Parma until 1818, when he was made
Duke of Reichstadt, the name by which
he is best known. Ranked just below
the Archdukes, he lived thereafter in
Vienna, where in 1832 in his gilded
palace of Schönbrunn he died at
twenty-one of lung disease.

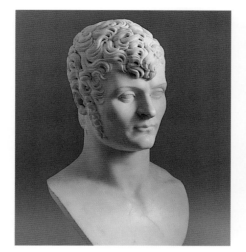

127

Workshops of Carrara,
after Antonio Canova
(1757–1822)

Caroline Bonaparte

Paris, Musée Marmottan-Claude Monet;
inv. 946
Marble
H. 70
First Empire

Napoleon's youngest sister Caroline was
born in Ajaccio in 1782. After trying to
better her education in Madame
Campan's school, in 1800 she married
Joachim Murat (1767-1815), a dashing
cavalryman utterly devoted to the
Emperor. The title of Imperial Highness
accorded to her by Napoleon was not
enough; she wanted a kingdom, but
the couple were assigned merely the
Grand Duchy of Berg and Clèves in 1806.
It was not until 1808 that they were
sent to govern in Italy, replacing Joseph
Bonaparte on the throne of Naples. Like
Louis in Holland, the Murats tried to win
an independence the Emperor was
unwilling to grant them. Caroline acted
as Regent when her husband was away.
Fearing the loss of his throne, Murat
approached the Allies in early 1814,
but he and Caroline decided to leave
Italy when the Hundred Days began.
After the execution of Murat, who had
attempted to regain his throne, Caroline
lived in Italy under the name of the
Countess of Lipona (an anagram of
Napoli) and died in Florence in 1839.

128

Possibly by Lorenzo Bartolini
(1777–1850),
after Joseph Chinard
(1756–1813)

**Jérôme Bonaparte, King of Westphalia,
after the statue in the city hall of Ajaccio**

Musée national des châteaux
de Malmaison et Bois-Préau;
MM 40–47–836;
Gift of Madame Raba Deutsch de la Meurthe
(formerly the collections of Napoleon III,
then of the Empress Eugénie)
Marble
H. 53
About 1810

Jérôme, the youngest of the family, was
born in Ajaccio in 1784. A carefree
lightweight, he was sent to sea by his
brother, serving in the Mediterranean and
the Atlantic. During leave in Baltimore in
1803 he was married, without Napoleon's
consent, to the young Elizabeth Patterson
whom he brought back to Europe
pregnant. After putting up a show of
resistance to his brother's orders Jérôme
had the marriage annulled. He was thus
brought back into the bosom of the
Imperial family, declared a Prince of France
and in 1807 married to Princesse Catherine
of Wurtemberg; that same year he was
made King of Westphalia, with Kassel his
capital. Jérôme was more concerned with
leading a life of pleasure than with
protecting a kingdom made up of ill-
assorted territories. In 1813 he had to leave
it and flee to France. After Waterloo where
he fought bravely he was exiled first to
Austria and then to Rome. When his
nephew Louis Napoleon seized power,
ushering in the Second Empire, Jérôme
was once again thrust on stage. He became
Governor of the Invalides, a Marshal of
France and president of the Senate, and
died in 1860 in his chateau at Villegenis,
near Paris.

132

Workshops of Carrara,
after
Antoine-Denis Chaudet
(1763–1810)

Napoleon I, crowned with laurel

Musée national des châteaux
de Malmaison et Bois-Préau;
MM 40–47–4365;
Gift of Comte Raoul Desmazières-Marchand,
1924 (grandson of the Emperor's man
servant on St. Helena, Louis Marchand)
Marble
H. 62
First Empire

In 1806 when the marble quarries
of Carrara came under the control
of the Emperor's sister Élisa she decided
to create an Academy under the Tuscan
professor of sculpture Lorenzo Bartolini
(1777-1850), who held the post from 1807
to 1814. The many sculptors under his
direction produced not only architectural
and decorative components but also
a large number of busts of Napoleon
and his family which Élisa sold at a
substantial profit. Almost all the official
busts of this period were made in
Carrara from original works by Chaudet,
Canova, Bosio and Chinard. It is estimated
that the workshop produced 12,000 busts
of Napoleon from Chaudet's model,
considered to be the official represen-
tation of the Emperor. The monumental
busts sold for 2,400 francs, the life-size
ones for 1,200 and the smallest for
between 500 and 600 francs.

133

Imperial factory of Sèvres:
Christophe-Ferdinand Caron
(1774–1831; active at Sèvres from 1792 to 1815);
Nicolas-Antoine Lebel
(active from 1804 to 1845);
Jacques-François-Joseph Swebach,
called Swebach-Desfontaines
(1769–1823; active from 1802 to 1813)

**Twenty-two-plate set of Archchancellor
Cambacérès with views of Italy and
the Fables of La Fontaine**
Private collection
Hard-paste porcelain
D. 23.5
1805 to 1807

This magnificent set of 22 plates is part
of the dessert service given by the Emperor
to his Archchancellor Jean-Jacques-Régis
de Cambacérès (1753-1824) on the occasion
of the marriage of Josephine's niece, the
Emperor's adoptive daughter Stéphanie
de Beauharnais, to the Crown Prince of
the Grand Duchy of Baden. The service is
remarkable for its glaze – a purple ground so
technically difficult to apply that the factory
did not repeat the process during the Empire
– and also for its original design, combining
views of Italy with depictions of the characters and animals of the *Fables* of La Fontaine.
Most of the views were taken from the
*Voyage pittoresque ou Description des
royaumes de Naples et de Sicile*, published
between 1781 and 1786 under the supervision
of the Abbé de Saint-Nom and from the
*Recueil de vues et fabriques pittoresques
d'Italie, dessinées d'après nature* by Constant
Bourgeois, published plate by plate from
1804 to 1808. The service went on sale at
the Sèvres factory on July 29, 1807 and was
delivered to Cambacérès on August 17
of the same year. It consists of 156 pieces
including 72 painted plates at 140 francs
each, a total of 10,080 francs for the plates
alone out of the 14,842 francs price for
the complete service.

Christophe-Ferdinand Caron

o- "The Eagle and the Owl."
year XIV (1806)

Jacques-François-Joseph Swebach

a- "n° 9 Waterfall of San Cosemato
The Fisherman and the Fish."
1807

Jacques-François-Joseph Swebach

b- "n° 10 View of the outskirts of Vietry near Salerno
The Donkey and the Peasant."
1807

Jacques-François-Joseph Swebach

c- "n° 11 View near the grottoes of San Pantorica
The Thieves and the Donkey."
1807

Jacques-François-Joseph Swebach

d- "n° 15 The Donkey and the Horse."
1807

Attributed to Christophe-Ferdinand Caron

e- "n° 26 The Lion and the Rat."
date obliterated

Nicolas-Antoine Lebel

f- "n° 32 View from Anagri, 45 miles from Rome."
year XIII (1805)

Jacques-François-Joseph Swebach

g- "n° 49 View of Castel Rozetto, Hither Calabria.
The Gardener and his Lord."
year XIV (1806)

Jacques-François-Joseph Swebach

h- "n° 51 Remains of antique tombs at Syracuse.
The Woodcutter and Death."
year XIV (1806)

Jacques-François-Joseph Swebach

i- "n° 54 View of the ruins of a temple to Castor and Pollux at Agrigento. The Gravedigger."
year XIV (1806)

Jacques-François-Joseph Swebach

j- "n° 58 View from Castro Giovani, the ancient villa of Enna, near the possible former site of the famous temple of Ceres. The Donkey and the Dog."
year XIV (1806)

Jacques-François-Joseph Swebach

k- "n° 59 View of a capital from the Temple of the Giants at Agrigento. The Lark, Her Babies and the Master of the Field."
year XIV (1806)

Jacques-François-Joseph Swebach

l- "n° 60 View of the Tower of Melissa in Calabria. Milk pitcher."
year XIV (1806)

Attributed to Nicolas-Antoine Lebel

m- "n° 65 View of an inn at Valmontone,
18 miles from Rome."
year XIV (1806)

Nicolas-Antoine Lebel

n- "n° 66 View of Tivoli, near Rome."
year XIV (1806)

Christophe-Ferdinand Caron

p- "The Hare and the Frogs."
year XIV (1806)

Attributed to Nicolas-Antoine Lebel

r- "Exterior view of a Capuchin church
at Siponto."
1807

Attributed to Nicolas-Antoine Lebel

s- "View of an Old Château built near LUCERA."
1807

Attributed to Nicolas-Antoine Lebel

t- "View of the Entrance to the Quarries
of Mount GARGANO."
1807

Nicolas-Antoine Lebel

u- "View of a villa near Monte-Mario, Rome."
1807

Attributed to Nicolas-Antoine Lebel

v- "Temple of Diana on the Seashore in
the Gulf of Baia."
1807

Nicolas-Antoine Lebel

q- "View of Trajan's Arch at Benevento."
1807

135

Box for transporting plates
Musée national des châteaux de Malmaison
et Bois-Préau; MM 67–8–1;
Gift of Baron Napoleon Gourgaud, 1967
Green Morocco leather, chamois leather, silk
H. 25; L. 29.5
1810

This is the only existing box of the six
used for transporting the plates from
the Emperor's famous personal service
of china, identifiable from the gilt swords
arranged round the green rims. Each box
held twelve of the seventy-two-plate-set,
the plates protected by leather discs tied
together by red cords tied in a pompon. This
box together with most of the service was
taken to St. Helena, and still shows the mark
of the Emperor's seal stamped there on
the island in 1821.

145

Place setting of Queen Hortense:

1 et 2- Pierre-Benoît Lorillon,
admitted as master-goldsmith in 1788, still working in 1836

Fork and spoon with Queen Hortense's monogram
Musée national des châteaux de Malmaison et Bois-Préau; MM 40–47–6890;
Gift of David David-Weill
Silver-gilt; Paris hallmarks for the period 1798–1809 and Lorillon's trademark
L. 19
First Empire, before 1809

4- Martin-Guillaume Biennais (1764–1843)

Knife with Queen Hortense's monogram
Musée national des châteaux de Malmaison et Bois-Préau; MM 40–47–6892;
Gift of David David-Weill
Silver-gilt; Paris hallmarks for the period 1798–1809, and Biennais's trademark
L. 20
First Empire, before 1809

5- Martin-Guillaume Biennais (1764–1843)

Fruit-knife with Queen Hortense's monogram
Musée national des châteaux de Malmaison et Bois-Préau; MM 40–47–6894;
Gift of David David-Weill
Silver-gilt, steel blade; Paris hallmarks for the period 1798–1809,
and Biennais's trademark
L. 10.2
First Empire, before 1809

3- Pierre-Benoît Lorillon,
master-goldsmith as of 1788, still working in 1836

Teaspoon with Queen Hortense's monogram
Musée national des châteaux de Malmaison et Bois-Préau; MM 40–47–6891;
Gift of David David-Weill
Silver-gilt; Paris hallmarks for the period 1798–1809, and Lorillon's trademark
L. 14.5
First Empire, before 1809

1

4   **2**

All these place-settings are from Queen Hortense's travelling case,
and went after her death in 1837 to her son the future Napoleon III.
The Empress Eugénie gave it to Firmin Rainbeaux, Napoleon's former
equerry, who bequeathed it to his son Félix Rainbeaux. David David-
Weill acquired this cutlery in 1936 in order to donate it to the Musée
de Malmaison.

144

Table napkin with Queen Hortense's monogram
Musée national des châteaux
de Malmaison et Bois-Préau;
MM 40–47–2035;
Gift of Madame Charles Floquet
Linen
H. 106; L. 93
About 1810

This napkin in a simple
damask weave bears an H
for Hortense embroidered
in red.

3   **5**

147

Nicolas-Antoine Lebel (active at Sèvres from 1804 to 1845)

Sugar bowl from the Emperor's private service:
"VIEW OF ELEPHANTINE ISLAND" AND "VIEW OF LUXOR"

Collection of Élaine Bédard - Alexandre de Bothuri Báthory
Hard-paste porcelain
W. 24
1810

This is one of the four "Etruscan" sugar bowls from the Emperor's private table service; the other three are in the Musée de Fontainebleau. The service, ordered in November 1807, comprised 72 plates depicting Napoleon's military campaigns, the museums and monuments of Paris, construction across the Empire, the imperial palaces and great institutions. It was delivered to the Tuileries on March 27, 1810; part of it was taken by Napoleon to St. Helena, and it is now scattered among various public and private collections. The four sugar bowls remained on the inventories of the Civil List until they were sold by the State after the fall of the Second Empire. The views of Luxor and Elephantine Island painted on this bowl are from the prints in *Voyage dans la Basse et la Haute Égypte*, published by Denon in 1802.

VUE DE L'ISLE ÉLÉPHANTINE.

138

Sugar spoon

Musée national des châteaux
de Malmaison et Bois-Préau
(Fonds Napoléon); N 75
Gift T.I.H. Prince Napoleon Bonaparte
and Countess de Witt, 1979
Silver
W. 10; L. 4.2
Late-18th century

According to tradition, this sugar spoon
was used by Napoleon between 1796
and 1821.

134

D. Garreau

Cruet stand

Collection of Élaine Bédard - Alexandre de Bothuri
Báthory
Silver; bears Paris hallmarks for
the period 1809–1819 and Garreau's mark
H. 33.3; L. 22.3; W. 11
About 1817–1819

The goldsmith Garreau specialised in making
cruets; he registered his own hallmark in 1817
and took over from Ambroise Mignerot in
1818. The hallmarks of title and warranty
correspond to the period 1809-1819; the cruet
stand can therefore be dated between 1817
and 1819. Although it undoubtedly dates
from the Restoration, it displays decorative
elements dear to the Empire, such as the
lion-claw feet and the cherubim riding on
a dog.

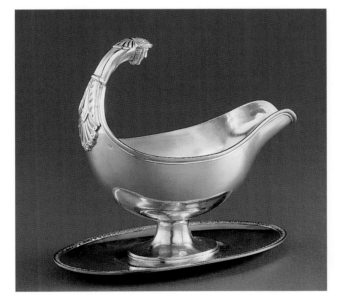

136

Anonymous

Glass cooler

New York, Malmaison Antiques
Silver plate
H. 16.5; L. 39.5; W. 22
Paris, early-19th century

Coolers for drinking-glasses in porcelain, earthenware, silver-plate or gold-plate appeared from the mid-18th century. They were made to cool several glasses at a time in ice, with the stems protruding outside; a cooler stood on a sideboard and chilled glasses were brought to table by waiters at the request of the diners. When in the 19th century glasses were placed directly on the table, these coolers disappeared or were used as planters.

137

Jacques-Brice Beaufort
(trademarks registered in 1788 and 1798–1806)

Sauceboat and saucer

Montreal, collection of the Honourable Serge Joyal, Senateur, P. C., C. O.
Silver; hallmarks of Paris 1798–1809 and of the master-gold-smith Jacques-Brice Beaufort
H. 21.2; L. 25.5
Paris, France; about 1798–1809

The raised rim is decorated with stylised palmette ribbing, and the handle formed of a superb head on a large palm-leaf.
R.D.

146

Louis Legeay
(active from 1810 to 1822)

Soup tureen

Montreal, collection of the Honourable
Serge Joyal, Senator, P. C., C. O.
Silver, alloy; Paris hallmarks for
1809–1819 and trademark of the Paris
master-goldsmith Louis Legeay
H. 36.5; W. 39
About 1815–1819

On this magnificent tureen we can
see obvious soldering at the bases
of the handles, and inside the bowl,
and under the scaling many
horizontal and vertical scratches
around each rivet of the handles.
R.D.

149

Possibly Claude Galle
(1759–1815)

Pair of pier tables with trophies and fasces
Private collection
Gilded bronze, mahogany, marble
H. 102; L. 72.2; W. 47.5
About 1804

It is thought that this remarkable pair of pier-tables were given by Napoleon to one of his aides-de-camp, General Jean-Léonor-François, Comte Le Marois (1783-1836) as a wedding present on his marriage in 1804 to Marie-Françoise-Constance Hopsomère (+ 1834). The attribution to the bronzesmith Claude Galle, one of Thomire's rivals, is based on similarities to the pair of candelabra with trophies and fasces delivered to Fontainebleau in 1805 and also to the wall-clock and standing clock with military trophies displayed in the exhibition of French industries held in 1806 (now in the Musée de Malmaison). Furniture made almost entirely of gilded bronze was rarely produced during the Empire.

140

Pierre-Philippe Thomire
(1751–1843)

Two pieces from an epergne
Montreal, Power Corporation
of Canada Collection;
inv. 1989.5.1.1–3 and 1989.5.1.4–6
Gilded bronze, crystal
H. 78; L. 41
Empire period

Thomire studied under
the sculptors Pajou and Houdon
and was recognised as the successor to the famous Gouthière. His
career began under the Ancien
Régime but took a spectacular
leap forward under the Empire,
when he was granted the title
"Manufacturer to His Imperial
and Royal Majesty". From his
workshops came innumerable
vases, fire-irons, clocks, candlesticks
and candelabra as well as many
epergnes or centrepieces for
the table. Each epergne consisted
of several components, most
signed "THOMIRE, PARIS"; they
could be candelabra, baskets,
flower-vases or fruit dishes, such as
these of crystal and gilt bronze.

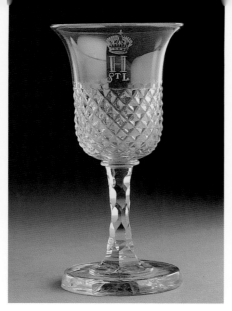

139

Attributed to the Montecenis
factory, Le Creusot

**Liqueur glass with Queen Hortense's
monogram**

Musée national des châteaux
de Malmaison et Bois-Préau;
MM 40–47–2063;
Gift of Mademoiselle Renée du Minil
H. 8.5; D. 5
About 1810

141

Attributed to the Montecenis
factory, Le Creusot

**Madeira glass with Queen Hortense's
monogram (inscribed: ST L, for Saint-Leu,
the Queen's residence near Paris)**

Musée national des châteaux
de Malmaison et Bois-Préau;
MM 40–47–2054;
Gift of Mademoiselle Renée du Minil
H. 11; D. 5.5
About 1810

142

Attributed to the Montecenis
factory, Le Creusot

**Champagne glass with Queen Hortense's
monogram**

Musée national des châteaux
de Malmaison et Bois-Préau;
MM 40–47–2064;
Gift of Mademoiselle Renée du Minil
H. 11; D. 5.5
About 1810

143

Attributed to the Montecenis factory, Le Creusot

Decanter with Queen Hortense's monogram

Musée national des châteaux de Malmaison et Bois-Préau;
MM 40–47–2080;
Gift of Mademoiselle Renée du Minil
H. 16.5; W. 7
About 1810

The Montecenis factory, established in Le Creusot, Burgundy in
the late-18th century to compete with English glassware, was run
under the Empire by Ladouèpe-Dufougerais and was sometimes
known by his name. Designated "Manufacturer of crystal to H.M.
the Empress", it made glassware and crystal components for
chandeliers for the imperial palaces. The factory closed its doors in
1832 when it was acquired by the firms of Baccarat and Saint-Louis.
Like her mother the Empress Josephine, Queen Hortense took her
business to this famous factory.

148

François, Baron Gérard
(1770–1837)

**Napoleon wearing the uniform
of the Grenadiers of the Imperial Guard**

Île d'Aix, Musée national de l'île d'Aix,
Fondation Gourgaud; M.G. A 207
Oil on canvas
H. 107; L. 70.5
Empire period

This portrait of Napoleon, unique in
Gérard's oeuvre, was commissioned to
be used as a model for the Paris mosaics
workshop directed after 1801 by the Rome
artist Francesco Belloni (1772-after 1840),
a renegade from the Vatican workshops.
Napoleon is wearing the uniform of the
Grenadiers of the Imperial Guard and,
unusually, the sword of the Egyptian
Institute. He is shown in an imaginary
setting, his hand resting on a table like
the Council tables, covered in papers.
Clearly the emphasis here is on Napoleon
the lawgiver, not Napoleon the soldier,
recalling his achievements as First Consul;
the youthful face harks back to that period.
Part of the mandate of the Imperial Mosaics
Factory was to reproduce paintings, on
the theory that mosaics last longer than
pictures. The copy of this work was begun
under the Empire but was left unfinished
after the events of 1814. Belloni worked on it
after 1830 and offered it, unsuccessfully, to
Louis-Philippe's government at the time
of the Return of the Ashes in 1840. Baron
de Nervo gave the mosaic to the Musée
de Malmaison in 1970, while Gérard's canvas
came to the Musée de l'île d'Aix, through
the generosity of Baron Gourgaud.

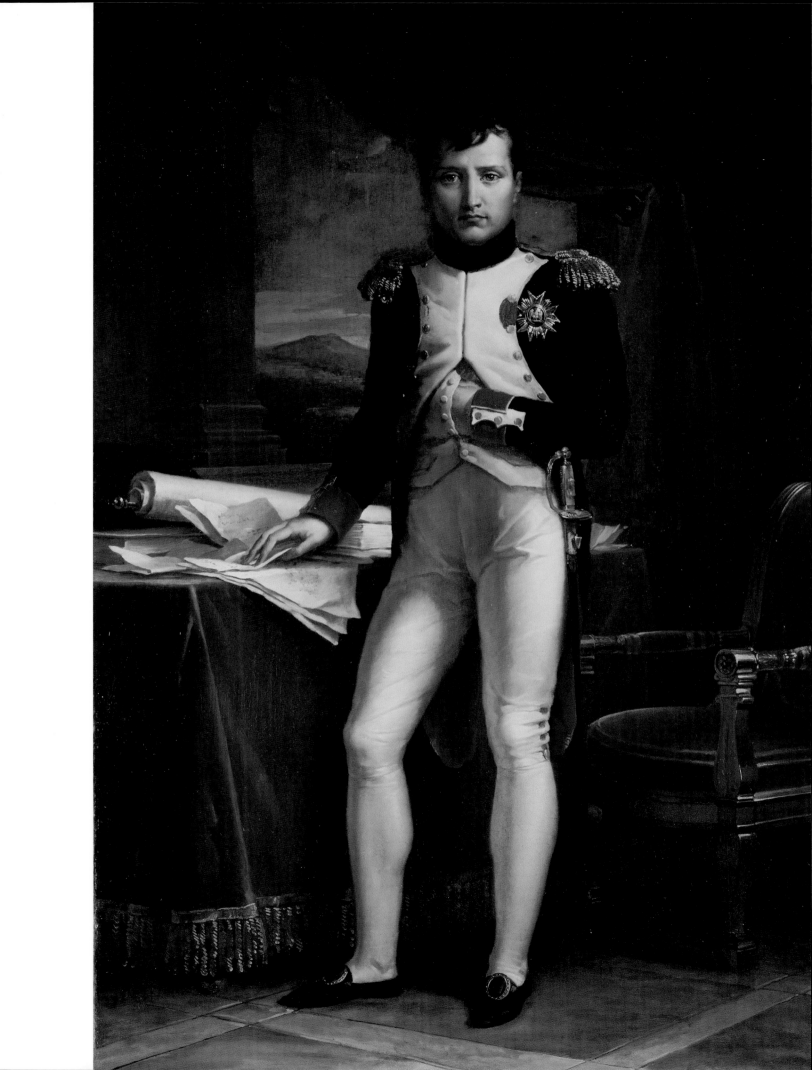

150

Daniel Saint (1778–1847)
for the miniature
Adrien-Jean-Maximilien
Vachette (1753–1839)
for the box

Portrait of Madame Cardon

Musée national des châteaux
de Malmaison et Bois-Préau;
MM 40–47–9874;
Gift of Edmé-Henri-Joseph-Jean,
Baron Rabusson-Corvisart, 1950
Miniature on ivory, gold, black lacquer,
glass; Vachette's trademark
H. 9.2; L. 6.3; W. 2.2
Empire period

Madame Cardon, the subject
of the painting, was the donor's
great-great-grandmother; her
daughter, Madame Augustin
de Lapeyrière, was also portrayed
by Saint during the Restoration.
Daniel Saint, who studied under
Isabey, Regnault and Aubry,
exhibited in the Salons from 1804
to 1839 and painted many
portraits of the Empress Josephine.
These miniatures on ivory could
be worn as brooches or pendants
or, as here, mounted on a box,
usually a gold box. This one bears
the trademark of the goldsmith
Adrien Vachette, accepted as
master-craftsman in 1779, who
specialised in this sort of item.

151

Pierre Bassereau
(about 1766–1808)

Duroc's watch

Musée national des châteaux
de Malmaison et Bois-Préau;
MM 73–2–25;
Gift of the descendents of Jacques
Coursot, the Emperor's butler
on St. Helena, 1973
Gold, enamel
D. 5.9; L. 8.2; W. 2.1
Empire period, before 1808

This watch's story is told in a
handwritten paper glued inside it:
"watch once belonging to Duroc,
Duke of Friuli, Grand Marshal
of the Palace to the Emperor
Napoleon I, killed in battle in 1813
at Wurtschen." Before the battle
Marshal Duroc entrusted his watch
to Jacques Coursot, the Emperor's
field secretary, with the words:
"If I come a cropper, you can keep
it." Christophe de Michel du Roc,
called Duroc (1772-1813), made
Duke of Friuli in 1808, was indeed
mortally wounded by a cannonball,
and Jacques Coursot (1786-1856)
inherited the watch that had been
left in his keeping. As he had no
heirs, it was bequeathed to his
nephew's many descendents, who
unanimously donated it, together
with precious souvenirs from
St. Helena, to the Musée
de Malmaison.

153

Smelling-salts bottle

Musée national des châteaux
de Malmaison et Bois-Préau;
MM 60–9–1;
Gift of Mrs Edith Holden
Crystal, gold
H. 8.6
Late-18th – early 19th century

This type of bottle was traditionally
used for smelling-salts, highly volatile
ammonium carbonate salts which
when inhaled revived fainting ladies.
This bottle first belonged to the
Empress Josephine. It was bequeathed
to her grandson Prince Louis Napoléon
Bonaparte, the future Emperor
Napoleon III, who gave it to Miss
Marguerite Power.

152

Pair of perfume-braziers
Musée national des châteaux
de Malmaison et Bois-Préau;
MM 40–47–7211 and 7212;
Gift of Madame Schmidt,
1935
Porcelain, gilded bronze
H. 45; L. 20
19th century

156

Mirror
Île d'Aix, Musée national de l'île d'Aix,
Fondation Gourgaud; M.G. 340
Gilded wood, mirror
H. 130; L. 83 (mirror: H. 82; L. 65)
19th century

155

Pierre Paraud,
active from 1800 to about 1813–1815
and Claude-René Ménessier,
active from 1826 to 1855

Pair of candlesticks
Montreal, collection
of the Honourable Serge Joyal,
Senator, P. C., C. O.
Silver; Paris hallmarks of
1798–1809 and 1819–1838 with those of
the master-goldsmiths Pierre Paraud
and Claude-René Ménessier. Both are
inscribed with the name
"THOUVENIN"
H. 27.7
About 1800–1809 and about 1819–1838

Each candlestick is decorated with
gryphons and interlacing on the frieze
around the base, claws at the base
of the stem, and vaguely Egyptian-
looking heads at the top of the stem.
R.D.

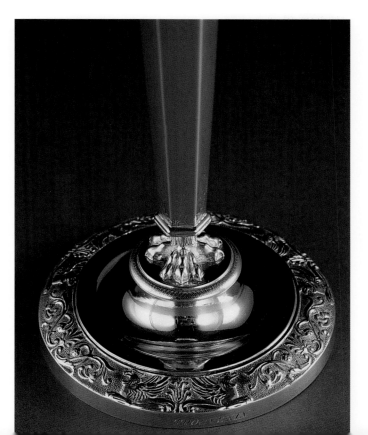

154

André-Antoine Ravrio
(1759–1814)

Pair of five-branch chandeliers

Musée national des châteaux
de Malmaison et Bois-Préau; MMD 60 [2];
(from the Mobilier national, 1991)
Gilded bronze
H. 75; L. 50
About 1805–1807

The bronzesmith Ravrio was one
of the main Suppliers of Furniture to
the Crown, and in that capacity provided
numerous clocks, chandeliers, candelabra
and sconces. Several pairs of chandeliers
were produced in his workshops, three
of them now in the Musée de Malmaison.
He provided similar sconces to most of
the imperial palaces such as Compiègne,
Meudon and the Tuileries. A pair with a
matte gilded finish might have cost
660 to 700 francs according to their size
while a pair with a simple varnish finish
cost only 325 francs. This pair has the
hallmark of the Tuileries Palace during
the Restoration.

158

Clock

Montreal, Power Corporation
of Canada Collection; inv. 1990.68.1
Gilded bronze, enamel.
Face signed: Jacquet à Gisors
H. 40.2; L. 37.6; W. 15.3
Early-19th century

This is an example of the architectural style
of clock. The movement is the work of a
Norman clockmaker, and the decoration
shows a combination of several influences.
The front pilasters are figures on plinths,
ending in the Egyptian nim, while the back
pilasters are winged victories in the Greek
style. The witty pendulum is an eagle
grasping a bee in its talons.

177

Ambroise-Louis Garnerey (1783–1857), after Auguste Garnerey (1785–1824)
View of the facade of the château from the park side
Musée national des châteaux de Malmaison et Bois-Préau; MM 40–47–4222;
Gift of Bernard Franck
Coloured aquatint on paper
H. 16; L. 23.5
About 1815–1820

On April 21, 1799 Josephine, hearing no news of Bonaparte who was detained in Egypt,
acquired the château of Malmaison ten kilometres west of Paris. The house, of no great
character, had been built in the early-19th century by a councillor of the parliament of Paris.
It owes the name of Malmaison (bad house) to the invasions of the 9th-century Vikings,
who set up camp there as a base from which they sallied forth to pillage and destroy the
surrounding villages.

Auguste Garnerey executed twelve watercolours of views of the Malmaison park which he
offered to Prince Eugène at the Restoration; his brother Louis Garnerey reproduced eight of
them at that time as aquatints to reach a wider market.

176

Ambroise-Louis Garnerey (1783–1857), after Auguste Garnerey (1785–1824)
View of the château, taken near the stone bridge over the lake
Musée national des châteaux de Malmaison et Bois-Préau; MM 40–47–4255;
Gift of Bernard Franck
Coloured aquatint on paper
H. 16; L. 23.5
About 1815–1820

After trying in vain to oppose the classical style of the gardens created under the
Consulate by Percier and Fontaine, in 1805 Josephine found at last in Louis-Martin
Berthault the landscape architect to redesign the park to her taste. Berthault, nicknamed
the Le Nôtre of the 19th century, broke new ground, in comparison with the Anglo-Chinese
gardens of the late-18th century, by greatly enlarging the prospects over the surrounding
countryside, fitting existing monuments into the viewpoints and limiting the number
of buildings. Thus the château of Saint-Germain, the church at Croissy and the Marly
aquaduct could be seen from the drawing-rooms of Malmaison. This is no longer the case,
since the great height of the trees blocks the view.

161

Victor-Jean Nicolle
(1754–1826)

**Monuments of Paris
(eight of fifty views)**

Musée national des châteaux
de Malmaison et Bois-Préau;
MM 40–47–9043 [6, 21, 38, 42, 45, 47, 48 et 50];
gift of Mr and Mrs John Jaffé, 1933
Watercolours on cardboard, signed and
inscribed on the back: "V.J. Nicolle Pinxit
[or] Delineavit"
H. 6.7; L. 11.7
About 1810

These eight watercolours are part
of a set of fifty views of Paris
commissioned from Nicolle for a
wedding gift for the new Empress,
Marie-Louise, to show her the
monuments of the capital over
which she was going to reign,
and especially the improvements
made under Napoleon's aegis, such
as bridges, fountains, markets and
new streets. His time studying with
the architect Petit-Radel induced
Nicolle to paint monuments, first in
Italy and later in Paris. The Empress
Josephine kept nineteen of his
views of Italy and six watercolours
of the palaces of Malmaison,
Saint-Cloud and Saint-Leu. This
remarkable set of fifty views of
Paris passed from Marie-Louise
into the Hapsburg family collection.
It was sold by the Archduke Franz-
Salvator, the Emperor Franz-Joseph's
son-in-law, and bought in 1933
for the Malmaison museum by an
Irish couple, Mr and Mrs. John Jaffé,
on the occasion of their diamond
wedding anniversary.

a

"View of the Monument raised
in Memory of General Desaix, and still
used as a public fountain in Paris,
Place Thionville"
MM 40–47–9043 [6]

b

"View of the Gallery of the Louvre,
taken from the Pont des Arts, Paris"
MM 40–47–9043 [21]

c

"View of the parterre and the Portal of
the Basilica of Notre-Dame, Paris"
MM 40–47–9043 [38]

d

"View of the Square and the City Hall,
City of Paris"
MM 40–47–9043 [42]

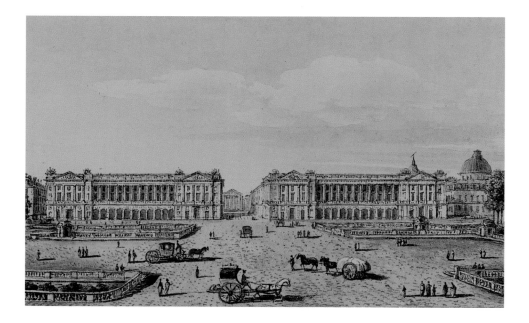

e

"View of the Place de la Concorde
fomerly of Louis XV and the buildings,
one serving as the Furniture Store
of the crown and the other as
the Ministry of the Navy, Paris"
MM 40–47–9043 [45]

f

"View of the Bellique Column
in the Place Vendôme, Paris"
MM 40–47–9043 [47]

g

"View of the Dome of the Imperial Church of the Invalides, taken from the noonday side, Paris"
MM 40–47–9043 [48]

h

"View of the frontispiece of the Palace of the legislative assembly, situated at the end of the Concorde Bridge, Paris"
MM 40–47–9043 [50]

Court cloak with train
Musée national des châteaux de Malmaison
et Bois-Préau (Fonds Napoléon); N 351;
purchase, 1979 (formerly the collections of the Imperial family)
Black silk velvet, gold, silver
H. 300; L. 135
First Empire

The Musée de Malmaison still has six of the Empress Josephine's
court trains from the Imperial family's collection or from
descendents of Prince Eugène. This black velvet mantle was
probably part of the 49 grand court robes listed in the inventory
of the Empress's wardrobe drawn up in 1809. Some of these
comprised a gown and matching cloak, others just a cloak with
a long train that was attached at the shoulders. The Anointing
cloak with the ermine lining no longer exists. It had been entrusted
along with that of the Emperor to the canons of Notre-Dame,
who sold it at the Restoration. Josephine's licensed dress
designer, the famous Leroy, was then the leader of fashion;
he was paid exactly half of what the Empress spent on her
appearance, and knew how to flatter his illustrious client,
who often invited him to the palace to discuss fabrics.

165

G.F. (unidentified goldsmith)

Teapot

Collection of Élaine Bédard - Alexandre
de Bothuri Báthory
Silver-gilt; hallmarks of Paris 1809–1819
and of a master-goldsmith G.F.
L. 28
About 1809–1819

This beautiful egg-shaped teapot has a base
engraved with palmettes; the short body
displays a band of garlands and military
and musical trophies inspired by the work
of Percier and Fontaine. The spout in
the shape of a dog's head is decorated
with acanthus leaves, and the lid is
surmounted by a pineapple.

166

Factory of Dihl and Guérhard

Teacup and saucer

Musée national des châteaux
de Malmaison et Bois-Préau;
MM 40–47–6120 and 6121;
gift of Madame Edmond Moreau
Hard-paste porcelain
Cup: H. 5; D. 9. Saucer: D. 13.5
Empire period

This cup and saucer was probably part
of a cabaret, the word used for breakfast,
tea, coffee and chocolate services. A cabaret
comprised, in addition to cups in sets of six,
twelve or more, a coffee-pot or teapot, a milk
jug, a cream jug, a sugar-bowl and a milk-
bowl that could also serve as a punch-bowl.
The shape of cups varied according to their
uses: coffee-cups were tall, of a shape called
"litron", teacups were lower and chocolate
cups more bulging. The Dihl and Guérhard
factory replaced the firm patronised by
the Duc d'Angoulême before the Revolution.
It became one of the finest in Europe under
the Empire, and was famous for the quality
of its gold work and the reputation of its
artists, including Demarne, Mallet, Drolling
and Swebach. This fine quality is apparent
even in simple pieces such as this teacup.

163

Covered candlestick

Musée national des châteaux de Malmaison et Bois-Préau;
MM 40–47–9752
Gilded bronze, sheet metal
H. 42; D. 14.2
Early-19th century

This sort of moveable lighting could be used in various ways:
on a desk, carried about or to shed light on a game of bouillotte,
hence the name of bouillotte-lamp sometimes used for the covered
candlestick. The height of the shade can be adjusted to the size
of the candle. Most covered candlesticks held several candles; this,
which has only one, appeared in the inventories of the Fontainebleau
palace in the 19th century.

164

Console-writing desk

New York, Malmaison Antiques
Mahogany, bronze
H. 86; L. 79.5; W.55
Early-19th century

This type of dual-purpose desk was
quite common under the Empire;
it could be placed between
the windows of a drawing-room
or bedroom, and when opened
became a writing desk with drawers
and a leather-covered flap. This is
a fairly rare example, as this sort
of combination-piece was usually
a commode, the wider surface
being easier to write upon.

157

Jean-Baptiste Gamichon (+ 1832)
Pier table
New York, Malmaison Antiques
Mahogany, bronze
H. 87.5; L. 112; W. 39
Empire period

This pier table, typical of the standard
output of the Paris workshops, carries the
stamp of Gamichon, whose career began
under Louis XVI and ended towards the close
of the Restoration. As a specialist in the
production of sideboards, chests of drawers,
writing desks and pier-tables, he was recom-
mended in 1811 to work in the Furniture Store
of the Crown, but his application seems to
have been turned down. In the exhibition of
1827 he showed products of French industry:
well-made furniture of maple, lemonwood
and amaranth, but the jury members did
not like them.

168

Antoine-Vincent Arnault (1766-1834), Antoine Jay (1770-1854), Victor-Joseph-Étienne, called de Jouy (1764-1846)

New Biography of Contemporaries or Historical and Systematic Dictionary of all the men who since the French Revolution have become famous for their actions, writings, errors or crimes, in France or in foreign countries, Paris, Librairie Historique, 1820 to 1825, 20 tomes in 8 volumes with the monogram of the Empress Marie-Louise.

Formerly the collection of the Empress Marie-Louise in Parma; sale of her library, Berlin, Martin Breslauer, January 17, 1933; Calvin Bullock Collection; Katherine Seymour Bullock Cole Bequest, New York sale, May 21, 1997.
Collection of Élaine Bédard - Alexandre de Bothuri Báthory
Leather, paper
Volume in-8°
1821 (for tome III) and 1823 (for tome IX)

The tomes selected contain entries on Bonaparte and the Empress Josephine; they are from the library of Marie-Louise when she reigned over the Duchy of Parma and ordered the purchase of almost everything published about the Empire and Napoleon.

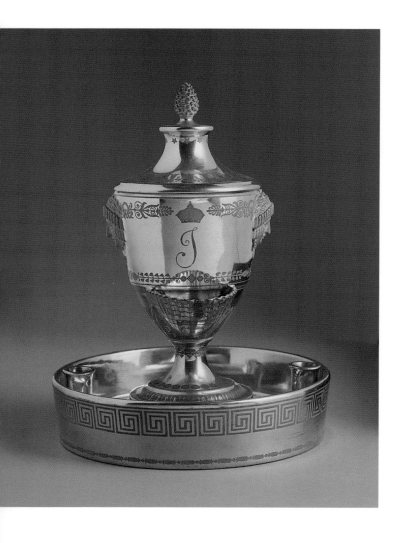

169

Dihl and Guérhard factory
Inkwell with the monogram of the Empress Josephine

Musée national des châteaux de Malmaison et Bois-Préau;
MM 76-4-1;
Gift of the Société des Amis de Malmaison
Hard-paste porcelain
H. 20; D. 15
About 1805

This inkwell was a gift from the Empress Josephine to the *landamann* (president) of Switzerland and *avoyer* (senior magistrate) of the canton of Berne, Nicolas-Rodolphe de Watteville, or von Wattenwyl (1760-1832), possibly during a trip she took to Savoie and Switzerland after her divorce; we know that on October 7, 1810 a grand dinner was given in her honour in Berne at the restaurant In der Enge by Madame de Watteville, and that gifts were exchanged on that occasion. Already in 1804 Josephine had given M. de Watteville a superb set of Sèvres porcelain to thank him for sending a herd of Bernese cows which she had housed in the cowsheds of Saint-Cucufa on the hillside near Malmaison. The inkwell remained with the descendents of M. de Wateville until one of them gave it to Colonel Sadi Carnot (1865-1948), the son of the President of the Republic and father of its last owner.

170

Daniel Saint
(1778–1847)

Box with a portrait of the Empress Josephine
Collection of Élaine Bédard - Alexandre de Bothuri Báthory
Tortoiseshell, ivory, gold
H. 2.5; L. 11; W. 4
Empire period

Saint was one of the great miniaturists, described in
the journal of the Empire in 1813: "M. Saint handles the
miniature in the grand manner introduced by M. Isabey and
as well as M. Isabey himself." He painted many portraits of
the Emperor and Empress for the service of the Cabinet. Like
Isabey, he was initially paid 500 francs for each work and
600 somewhat later; the miniatures were then mounted
on boxes of varying degrees of richness, those sporting
diamonds being most often made by the goldsmith Nitot.
The artist was not required to capture a perfect likeness:
on the topic of miniaturists Daru, quartermaster general
of the House of the Emperor, wrote: "Advise them to paint
fairly amiable faces." Josephine wears here her set of pearls:
a tiara, a necklace of eight large pear-shaped gems and a
pair of earrings. The box was part of the collection of
Sir John Murray Scott (+ 1913), secretary to Sir Richard
Wallace, who was famous for the art collection bequeathed
to England by his widow.

171

Martin-Guillaume Biennais
(1764–1843)

Milk jug with the arms of Napoleon and Marie-Louise
Montreal, Ben Weider Collection
Silver-gilt; Paris hallmarks for the period 1809–1819
and Biennais's stamp
H. 18.2
Between 1810–1814

In addition to his "Grand Vermeil", presented to him by
the city of Paris on the occasion of his coronation and only
used on state occasions, the Emperor also used a simpler
silver-gilt service and a sterling silver one, both sets being
continually completed and rearranged. Biennais was the
official goldsmith of the imperial tableware. In 1811 he
delivered items costing a total of 720,199 francs: 46 dishes,
38 candelabras,10 soup tureens, 62 dishcovers and several
hundred plates. This milk jug with the coats of arms of
Napoleon and Marie-Louise seems rather to have come
from a travelling case (such cases held more or fewer items
depending on their use); the most luxurious one, given to
the Empress by the city of Paris and also made by Biennais,
held no less than 77 pieces (now in the Schatzkammer,
Munich).

172

Ambroise-Louis Garnerey (1783–1857), after Auguste Garnerey (1785–1824)

View of the park taken from the château

Musée national des châteaux de Malmaison et Bois-Préau; MM 40-47-4236;
Gift of Bernard Franck
Coloured aquatint on paper
H. 16; L. 23.5
About 1815–1820

Once Malmaison was purchased, Josephine gave her full attention to the park. She wanted
everything to be in the English manner and would not tolerate a single straight path; a
walk leading directly from one place to another she considered barbarous, a crime against
the rules of artistic gardening. Her projects were endless: she wanted to see little temples,
tombs and rocks, everything that Percier and Fontaine considered the idiocies of English-
style gardening. Four architects came and went in five years before the Empress found
in Louis-Martin Berthault (1770-1823) the architect who could carry out all her notions. He
understood her wishes so well that he remained in her service until her death. Berthault
redesigned the park, embellished it with structures and created an artificial stream
adorned with rock bridges and a grotto.

184

Ambroise-Louis Garnerey (1783–1857) after Auguste Garnerey (1785–1824)

View from the wooden bridge over the stream, to the left of the château

Musée national des châteaux de Malmaison et Bois-Préau; MM 40–47–4256;
Gift of Bernard Franck
Coloured aquatint on paper
H. 16; L. 23.5
About 1815–1820

From the small stream that trickled down from the pool of Saint-Cucufa, Berthault tried
to create an English river that could take small craft. It was crossed by several wood or
stone bridges, and the variations in height solved with the help of many waterfalls made
of piled-up rocks. The banks were planted with rare species. Despite all this labour, the
water-level was always dropping, leaving the rock faces covered in clay.

174

François-Honoré-Georges
Jacob-Desmalter (1770–1841)

Drawing-room chair
Montreal, Power Corporation
of Canada Collection;
inv. 1990.257.1.1
Gilded wood; stamp
of Jacob-Desmalter
H. 98.7; L. 61; W. 61
Consulate period

The workshops of Jacob-Frères
and later those of Jacob-Desmalter
made many ceremonial chairs
of this sort, often with slight
variations in style depending on
the commission. One of them can
be seen in the portrait of the First
Consul by Ingres; the inventories
of the imperial palaces record that
Jacob-Desmalter made them for
the château of Laeken in Belgium,
for the Empress's apartments in
the palace of Compiègne, for the
Emperor's great hall in the Grand
Trianon and for the council chamber
at Malmaison. This chair is very like
them, though lacking the two
lions' mouths at the ends of the
armrests.

175

Attributed to François-Honoré-
Georges Jacob-Desmalter
(1770–1841)

Tea table

Musée national des châteaux
de Malmaison et Bois-Préau;
MM 40–47–103
(from the Mobilier national)
Mahogany, painted marble
H. 73; D. 67
About 1805

This tea table came from the
furniture ordered by Murat for
the Élysée palace. After coming
into possession of the palace on
August 6, 1805 he lost no time in
ordering 390,000 francs worth of
furniture from the firm of Jacob.
On being made King of Naples
in 1808, Murat had to give up the
Élysée to the Emperor, but the
table appears in the inventory
of 1809 in the small sitting-room of
his apartment. In 1810 during the
divorce Napoleon gave the life-
interest and possession of the
Élysée to Joséphine; she did not
keep it long, being obliged to give
it back to the Emperor in 1812. It
was there that Napoleon spent
most of the Hundred Days,
and that he signed his second
abdication on June 22, 1815, before
leaving for Malmaison, the Île d'Aix
and finally St. Helena, where he
found the tea table in the second
drawing-room of his small
apartment.

178

Imperial factory of Sèvres: Jean-Marie-Ferdinand Régnier
(1774–1857), active at Sèvres from 1812 to 1814 and from 1820 to 1848

Régnier breakfast service in relief comprising five pieces: teapot, cup for chocolate, bowl, milk jug and sugar bowl

Sèvres, Musée National de Céramique; inv. MNC 6160;
Gift of Emperor Napoleon III, 1856
Hard-paste porcelain; hallmark of the Sèvres factory
stamped on the glaze, in red for the years 1813–1815
Teapot, H. 15.5; cup for chocolate, H. 10, D. 8.6; its saucer, D. 15.4;
bowl, D. 15.8; milk jug, H. 11; sugar bowl, H. 13.5, D. 9.7
1813

This exquisitely elegant breakfast service designed by Ferdinand Régnier in 1813 is unusual
for Sèvres production under the First Empire, its technique heralding the style that would
become fashionable in the 1830s. The matte gold ground is directly applied on the bisque;
only some components and the inside of the pieces are lined with brilliant gold on the
enamelled parts. This technique emphasises the rich decoration of white bisque, borrowed
from ancient times, that takes up all the available space. The idea was doubtless taken from
the jasperware technique perfected by the English firm of Wedgewood, gold here replacing
the famous Wedgewood blue. On January 1, 1814 this service, which cost 945 francs, was
given as a New Year's gift by Napoleon to the Duchess of Castiglione, née Adélaïde-
Joséphine Bourlon de Chavange (1789-1869), wife of Marshal Augereau.

180

Garden table with moveable marble top
Musée national des châteaux de Malmaison et Bois-Préau; MM 51–1–19;
Gift of Baroness Napoléon Gourgaud (née Eva Gebhard) 1951
Mahogany, gilded bronze, green marble
H. 84; D. 35
Early-19th century

173

Ambroise-Louis Garnerey (1783–1857), after Auguste Garnerey (1785–1824)

View of the stucco room in the greenhouse

Musée national des châteaux de Malmaison et Bois-Préau; MM 40–47–4223;
gift of Bernard Franck
Coloured aquatint on paper
H. 16; L. 23.5
About 1815–1820

Josephine's passion for botany led her into considerable expenditure; the most costly
project was undoubtedly the great greenhouse. This remarkable 50-metre-long building
was heated by twelve coal-fired stoves, and, as it was completely glassed in, made it
possible to grow plants five metres high. Behind the actual hothouses was a row of
sitting-rooms luxuriously decorated by the architect Berthault, which gave delightful
views of the plants. The Empress personally supervised additions to her botanical collection;
it was at Malmaison that almost 200 new plants were first cultivated in France. The
glasshouses were soon demolished, but the main building was converted into a residence
and still contains the sumptuous sitting-rooms suggested by Josephine.

183

Ambroise-Louis Garnerey (1783–1857), after Auguste Garnerey (1785–1824)

View of Neptune's basin outside the park near the railings

Musée national des châteaux de Malmaison et Bois-Préau; MM 40–47–4224;
Gift of Bernard Franck
Coloured aquatint on paper
H. 16; L. 23.5
About 1815–1820

The road outside the enclosed park led up to Neptune's basin, an old storage tank restored
by Berthault in 1807. He provided it with a marble statue formerly attributed to Puget and
two rostral columns from the demolished château de Richelieu in Poitou, once the
residence of Louis XIII's Cardinal-minister.

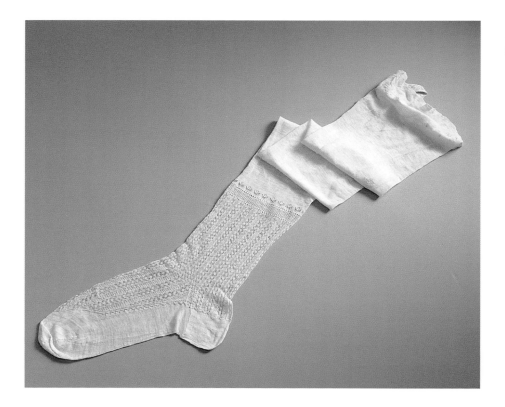

182

Stocking of the Empress Josephine

Musée national des châteaux
de Malmaison et Bois-Préau;
MMD 25/2;
(from the Musée national du Moyen Âge),
1957
White linen thread
L. 74
First Empire

Clothes were the Empress's whole life,
and since the Continental Blockade
had stopped the importing of English
merchandise she did not hesitate to
have items smuggled into France,
often making use of her relatives.
Some packages seized by the French
customs were claimed in the Empress's
name but immediately destroyed by
order of the Emperor; this did not stop
her from trying again, desperate for the
forbidden fruit. The inventory of 1809,
for example, shows that she owned
498 shifts, 1,132 pairs of stockings,
785 pairs of shoes and 676 gowns.
There were 413 pairs of stockings of
silk or cotton, and that same year she
purchased 71 pairs. At her death in 1814
there were still 269 pairs left in the
dressing-room at Malmaison.

179

François-Honoré-Georges
Jacob-Desmalter
(1770–1841)

Footstool

New York, Malmaison Antiques
Gilded wood
H. 16; L. 45; W. 38
Early-19th century

181

François-Honoré-Georges Jacob-Desmalter (1770–1841),
after a drawing by Charles Percier (1764–1838)

Boudoir chair of the Empress at the palace of Saint-Cloud (from a set of four)

Musée national des châteaux de Malmaison et Bois-Préau; MM 40–47–942
(from the Mobilier national)
Painted wood and gilded wood, red silk velvet, gold
H. 77; L. 66; W. 51
About 1804

This chair was part of a set of furniture made by Jacob for Josephine's boudoir at the palace
of Saint-Cloud. This former house of Queen Marie-Antoinette by the gates of Paris had been
offered to the First Consul, who took up residence there in the fall of 1802. The four chairs,
now in the Musée de Malmaison, were among the most original creations of the period, made
from a design by the architect Percier; the swan-shaped armrests have a graceful appearance
thereafter associated with Josephine's memory. They have recently been re-covered in gold-
embroidered red velvet as they were originally.

160

Ambroise-Louis Garnerey (1783–1857), after Auguste Garnerey (1785–1824)

View of the sheepfold in the wood as you leave the park

Musée national des châteaux
de Malmaison et Bois-Préau;
MM 40–47–4237;
Gift of Bernard Franck
Coloured aquatint on paper
H. 16; L. 23.5
About 1815–1820

The sheepfold was a building almost 90 metres long on the hillside halfway between
the château and the pool of Saint-Cucufa. It was begun in 1805 by the architects Thibault
and Vignon but the surface area was doubled in 1806-1807 by Louis-Martin Berthault,
architect at Malmaison from 1805 until the death of the Empress. The sheepfold held
merino sheep, more than two thousand of them in 1812. It disappeared completely during
the Franco-Prussian War of 1870-1871.

159

Ambroise-Louis Garnerey (1783–1857), after Auguste Garnerey (1785–1824)

View of the cowshed in the woods at Saint-Cucufa

Musée national des châteaux
de Malmaison et Bois-Préau;
MM 40–47–4254;
Gift of Bernard Franck
Colour aquatint on paper
H. 16; L. 23.5
About 1815–1820

In 1801 Josephine enlarged her estate at Malmaison by purchasing the pool of
Saint-Cucufa in the depths of the woods of the same name. In 1804 on the banks
of the pool Jean-Marie Morel (1728-1810) the Malmaison architect built in 1804 these
three small buildings: a house for the shepherd, a dairy and a cowshed, which also housed
the two Swiss cowherds and the ten beasts presented to the Empress by the town of
Berne. Now very much transformed, they still stand in a semicircle around the west bank
of the pool.

Rosa Sulfurea.   Rosier jaune de soufre.

185

Pierre-Gabriel Langlois
(1754-about 1810),
after Pierre-Joseph Redouté
(1759–1840)

Sulphur-yellow rose bush

Musée national des châteaux
de Malmaison et Bois-Préau;
MM 40–47–587
Engraving tinted with watercolour
H. 35; L. 26
1817–1824

Joséphine's passion for botany led her
to transform Malmaison into a real
experimental garden, a rival to the
garden of the Natural History Museum.
She had a number of books published
at her own expense with reproductions
of the plants at Malmaison, which she
had commissioned from Pierre-Joseph
Redouté, called the Raphaël of flowers.
Her collection of roses came to almost
250 different varieties which she asked
Redouté to paint. The Empress's death
delayed publication: the three volumes
of the work from which these plates are
taken were not published until the years
1817 to 1824, first in twenty-seven
instalments and later bound. It was
common in the First Empire to give the
same rose several names; one variety
often had up to ten names.

Rosa centifolia.   Rosier à cent feuilles.

186

Couten, after Pierre-Joseph
Redouté (1759–1840)

Hundred-leaf rose bush

Musée national des châteaux
de Malmaison et Bois-Préau;
MM 40–47–584
Engraving tinted with watercolour
H. 35; L. 26
1817–1824

The hundred-leaf rose was propagated
by André Dupont's rival Descemet, a
nurseryman who was also the mayor
of Saint-Denis; in 1815 he owned almost
ten thousand young rose bushes raised
from seed, a considerable number at
the time.

187

**Pair of mules embroidered with
the initials EB**

Montreal, The Stewart Museum at the Fort,
Île Sainte-Hélène; inv. 1970.100.71
Leather, silk velvet, metallic thread
France
About 1805

This pair of mules embroidered with
the initials EB and golden imperial bees
may have belonged to Eugène de
Beauharnais, the Empress Josephine's
son and step-son to Napoleon, who
made him Viceroy of Italy and a Prince
of the Empire. He distinguished himself
in the Emperor's campaigns.
G.V.

V

1804-1815

Commander of the Grand Army

188

Jean-Baptiste-Claude-<u>Eugène</u> Guillaume
(1822–1905)

Napoleon I in 1812

Musée national des châteaux
de Malmaison et Bois-Préau;
MM 40–47–6846;
Gift of Madame Henri Lefuel,
descendent of the sculptor
Plaster
H. 73; L. 60
Second Empire

This bust is one of a series of six
sculpted portraits of Napoleon at
different stages of his life.

Not being sprung from a race of kings, Napoleon could remain in power only through
further victories, and the governments of Europe had been making alliances against
France since England broke the peace of Amiens in October 1803. After the
destruction of the French fleet at Trafalgar (October 21, 1805) Bonaparte could
not invade England by sea, so he decided to attack his enemies on land. From the
summer of 1805 he had to contend with England, Austria, Russia, Sweden and
Naples, but his shattering victory at Austerlitz (December 2, 1805) enabled him to
dictate conditions to his opponents. Russia, England and Prussia, only just beaten,
formed a fourth alliance against France but the King of Prussia and the Czar,
subdued by their losses at Jena and Auerstadt (October 1806) and the defeat at
Eylau (February 1807), resigned themselves to signing a peace with Napoleon.
The Emperor was now free to redraw the map of Europe as he liked, handing out
kingdoms to his nearest and dearest: brother Joseph to reign in Naples and brother
Louis in Holland, and later brother Jérôme got Westphalia while Murat took over
Naples from Joseph who went to rule in Spain. In 1811 the Great Empire comprised
130 departments or administrative regions, Rome becoming chief city of the
department of Tiber and Amsterdam of the Zuyder Zee. The electors of Bavaria,
Wurtemberg and Saxony, Napoleon's allies, were raised to kingly rank.

In November 1806, unable to defeat England by force of arms Napoleon attempted to
starve her economically by decreeing a continental blockade. To ensure that it was
strictly enforced he was obliged to make further conquests to make sure of the
Baltic ports, Portugal and even Spain. But the Grand Army would become bogged
down in a guerilla war against the Spanish people which was to keep 300,000 of
Napoleon's best troops uselessly occupied until 1814.

Taking advantage of the difficulties faced by the French in Madrid, Austria entered into
a fifth coalition with England and resumed hostilities in April 1809. The victory of
Wagram opened the gates of Vienna to Napoleon for the second time, and Austria
was forced to cede more territories.

Aware of the precarious nature of his regime, Napoleon longed to ensure the continuity
of his line by separating from Josephine, who could not give him an heir. He finally
decided on divorce and accepted the marriage with the Archduchess Marie-Louise

of Austria proposed to him by her father, the Emperor Francis I (April 2, 1810). Gratified by this alliance with the Hapsburgs, the Emperor discovered a new youthfulness, made manifest the following year in the birth of the longed-for heir, the King of Rome (March 20, 1811). The Empire appeared to be at its apogee, but the enemy nations were in reality more subdued than conquered.

Hostilities commenced with the Czar, unhappy at the creation of the Grand Duchy of Warsaw, and Napoleon, vexed with Alexander for not enforcing the Continental Blockade. War was declared on June 22, 1812 and the odds seemed with Napoleon, who was bringing 600,000 men against the Czar's 250,000. Adopting a scorched-earth policy, the Russians retreated before Napoleon's troops into the interior, avoiding combat as much as possible; on September 14 the Emperor entered Moscow – a city in flames. Realising that Alexander would not sue for peace, he rapidly ordered the retreat. Tortured by hunger and thirst in the grip of the bitter Russian winter, the army was reduced to a long column of fugitives of whom only a few thousand survived to cross the Berezina on November 29, 1812. The Emperor returned hastily to Paris: almost nothing was left of the Grand Army.

Heartened by this, the King of Prussia entered into an alliance with the Czar against France; this was the start of the fifth coalition, which brought together Russia, Prussia, England and Austria. After the French defeat at the battle of Leipzig, called the Battle of the Nations (October 15, 1813), former allies of Napoleon from the kings of Bavaria and Wurtemberg to Murat and Bernadotte began to defect in the hope of keeping their kingdoms. The end of 1813 saw Spain lost, together with Napoleonic Germany and Holland, while Italy was ready to fall into the hands of the Austrians (April 1814).

For the first time in ten years the war focused on France, relinquishing the borders of the Empire. It was now a question of preventing an invasion of France herself and of saving Paris. Despite a remarkable stand by the French, during which Napoleon rediscovered the tactical genius of General Bonaparte, the Allied armies entered Paris on March 31, 1814, the capitulation having been signed by Marmont that same night. The Emperor retired to Fontainebleau and on April 6, urged to it by his Marshals, signed his first abdication and set off into exile.

Made ruler of the island of Elba off the coast of Italy, Napoleon took his job seriously, reorganising his little kingdom of twelve thousand inhabitants and setting up a semblance of the Imperial court together with his mother and his sister Pauline, as the Empress Marie-Louise had stayed in Vienna with her son, the King of Rome. Knowing of the growing unrest in France since his departure and of the Bourbons' unpopularity, Napoleon decided to cast the die, setting sail for France on February 26, 1815. In twenty days with seven hundred men he reconquered France, coming home on March 20, 1815 to the Tuileries palace which Louis XVIII had scarcely had time to leave. Although Napoleon was supported by the peasants and the working classes, the middle and upper classes either shunned him or were outright hostile. He established a liberal Empire to reassure public opinion in a France worn out by incessant war, but his coup lasted only a Hundred Days, as the Allies gathered in Vienna had banned him from Europe and decided to fight him until he was defeated once and for all.

Since he had to fight, the Emperor took the offensive and entered Belgium in the hope of crushing Wellington's Anglo-Prussian forces. But on June 18, 1815 the battle of Waterloo destroyed his hopes, ending in an absolute disaster and the rout of the French army. Returning to Paris Napoleon abdicated on June 22 from the Élysée palace in favour of his son the King of Rome, and was swiftly replaced on the throne by Louis XVIII who had come back from Ghent, Belgium.

203

Poupard and Delaunay, hatter at Paris

Hat belonging to the Emperor

Musée national des châteaux
de Malmaison et de Bois-Préau
(Fonds Napoléon); N 291;
Gift of T.I.H. the Prince and Princess Napoléon
Bonaparte (formerly the collection of
the Imperial family)
Felt, silk
H. 25; l. 42
About 1814–1815

The famous little cocked hat was so closely
associated with the Emperor's image that
it became its symbol. We know that he was
already wearing one like this during his
Consulate and throughout his reign never
changed the style. His hats were made of
black felt, without trimming or braid, adorned
with a simple tricolour cockade held in place
with a black cord. Napoleon wore his cocked
hat "broadside on", the brim aligned with
the shoulders, whereas officers usually
wore theirs "fore-and-after". Each hat cost
60 francs and the trim 12; they were made
by the hatter Poupard, later Poupard and Co.
in 1808 and then Poupard and Delaunay
in 1811, at the sign of the "Temple of Taste", in
the Palais Royal. The existing bills suggest
that the firm made some 170 hats for
Napoleon in the course of his career; about
twenty of those existing are of undisputed
provenance. The Emperor had only four hats
left on St. Helena: one was placed in his
coffin, another bequeathed to Queen Caroline
and the remaining two, including this one,
were given to the Comte de Montholon and
to Marchand, the Emperor's valet.

189

Uniform of an officer of the Dragoons of the Imperial Guard

Salon-de-Provence, Château-Musée de l'Empéri (formerly the Raoul and Jean Brunon Collection)

The Dragoons played a variety of roles, serving in the heavy as well as the light cavalry. They carried a long rifle, and sometimes fought on foot. Dragoons wore a helmet similar to the Cuirassiers' but of copper and embellished with leopard skin or sealskin. They wore leather overalls, as did the men of the heavy cavalry.

190

Uniform of an officer of the Hussars, 5th regiment

Salon-de-Provence, Château-Musée de l'Empéri (formerly the Raoul and Jean Brunon Collection)

Hussars and Chasseurs à cheval together formed the light cavalry, whose business was scouting for the army, reconnaissance, pursuit and harassment of the enemy, activities that required special qualities of endurance and initiative together with great daring. Hussars with their dashing Hungarian-style uniforms were the most colourful horsemen in the army. Each of the fourteen regiments had its own colours (regimental flags).

191

Uniform of a fusilier of the Line Infantry, 6th regiment

Salon-de-Provence, Château-Musée de l'Empéri (formerly the Raoul et Jean Brunon Collection)

The infantry, as in any century, were the backbone of the Grand Army. It is the foot soldier who gets the longest hardest job. With his cow-hide pack on his back and his rolled cape on top of it, carrying his long gun made even longer with the bayonet fixed, he legged it through every country in Europe, from the sierras of Spain to the Russian steppes.

Dragoons of the Imperial Guard

Hussars, 5th regiment

Fusilier of the Line Infantry, 6th regiment

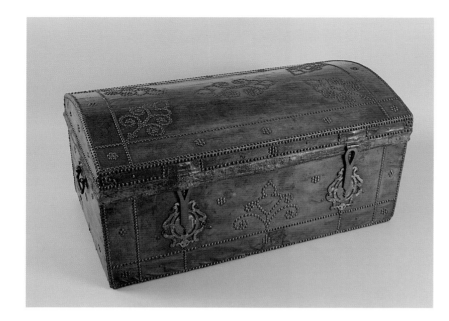

Junot's trunk

Musée national des châteaux
de Malmaison et Bois-Préau;
MM 40-47-4090;
Gift of Madame Bethemont, 1913
Leather, copper
H. 55; L. 110; W.3
Early-19th century

This trunk, probably of Portuguese
manufacture, is designed to fit into a
travelling carriage. It belonged to Andoche
Junot (1771-1813), a boyhood friend of the
Emperor, who in 1800 appointed him
governor of Paris. Then he was made
ambassador to Portugal in 1805, was ordered
by Napoleon to invade that country in 1807,
and became its governor-general for a brief
while before having to surrender to the
future Duke of Wellington in August 1808.
Napoleon made him Duke of Abrantès the
following year but Junot soon went mad
and in 1813 killed himself by jumping out of
a window. He was never made a Marshal.

193

Sapper's axe

Montreal, The Stewart Museum at the Fort,
Île Sainte-Hélène;
inv. 1973.18.13
Steel, wood
H. 95; W. 42.5 (2.8 kg)
France; about 1805

Sappers were soldiers in the engineering
corps whose main task was to dig the
trenches and passageways by which enemy
fortifications could be approached: this was
the "sap work" from which the name came.
Once the fortifications were reached they
laid explosive charges, mines, under the walls
to blow it up and make a breach. On parade
sappers were recognisable by their axes,
carried proudly, their big white leather
aprons and their long beards.
G.V.

194

Coulaux Frères, directors of
the Imperial factory at Klingenthal

French short sword

Montreal, The Stewart Museum at the Fort,
Île Sainte-Hélène; inv. 1968.4
Steel, brass
H. 74
France; about 1805

The short sword traditionnally used by the
infantry is about 74 cm long with a curved
profile. It was worn by men in the élite
companies, junior officers and corporals.
The sword used by the old guard had a
slightly longer blade.
G.V.

196

Attributed to Nicolas-Noël Boutet
(1761–1833), director of the Versailles
munitions factory

**Sword of a dignitary of the Empire,
once belonging to Marshal Ney**

Paris, Musée de l'Armée; inv. J 25151;
Purchase, 1983
Gilded bronze, mother-of-pearl, steel, shagreen
L. 84
Empire period

Several swords of this type are known to
have belonged to Marshals of the Empire.
This one, the property of Marshal Ney, was
part of the collection of his descendents the
princes of Moskova. Michel Ney (1769-1815)
was the son of a cooper in Sarrelouis,
Lorraine. He enlisted at the age of 18, moved
swiftly up the ladder of promotion and was
a general by 1799. His marriage to a school-
friend of Hortense de Beauharnais brought
him in contact with Napoleon, who included
him in the first batch of marshals in 1804.
Ney, "the bravest of the brave", was in every
battle, and the Emperor first made him
Duke of Elchingen (1808) and later Prince
of Moskova (1813). After urging Napoleon to
abdicate he joined Louis XVIII, promising
to bring back the Emperor in an iron cage
after his escape from Elba. In fact he flung
himself into his old master's arms, and this
change of heart brought him, after the
second Restoration, to trial; he was con-
demned for high treason, and shot in 1815.

195

(Anonymous)

Portrait of Marshal Macdonald

Montreal, The Stewart Museum at the Fort,
Île Sainte-Hélène; inv. 1973.18.3
Oil on canvas
H. 88.6; L. 69.7
France

Étienne-Jacques Macdonald, born in Sedan
on November 17, 1765 of a Scottish family
settled in France in the mid-18th century, had
a brilliant career. He was a brigadier-general
by 1793, major-general by 1794 and a Marshal
of the Empire following the victory of
Wagram in 1809. That same year he was
made Duke of Tarento. He was captured at
the battle of Leipzig and made his way back
to the French camp *in extremis* after
swimming the Elster river. Macdonald rallied
to Louis XVIII's cause in 1814 and held himself
aloof from the Hundred Days. He is said to
have been a calm, stubborn, serious character
with a cold manner who had trouble
communicating with his men. He died at
Courcelles on September 25, 1840.
G.V.

197

Jean, called John, Godefroy (1771–1839), after François, Baron Gérard (1770–1837)

The Battle of Austerlitz

Musée national des châteaux de Malmaison et Bois-Préau; MM 58-3-42 bis;
Gift of Princess George of Greece, 1958 (formerly the Demidoff Collection,
Prince of San Donato, later to Prince Roland Bonaparte, the donor's father)
Black and white engraving on paper
H. 55; L. 97.7
1813

Austerlitz was undoubtedly one of the most brilliant and decisive victories ever achieved
by French troops. The battle, sometimes known as the Battle of the Three Emperors, took
place on December 2, 1805, a year to the day after the coronation; 65,000 of Napoleon's
men beat the 90,000 soldiers of the Emperors of Austria and Russia. The Allied forces
lost 15,000 men killed or wounded and 20,000 taken prisoner, 45 regimental flags and
186 cannons, while the French army had only 800 killed and 7,000 wounded. Austerlitz
forced the Allies to ask for armistice. This print depicts the moment when General Rapp
reported to the Emperor that he had repulsed the attack by the Russian army. The original
painting was commissioned from Gérard for the Tuileries; it was shown at the Salon of
1810, and after being enlarged was installed in the reign of Louis-Philippe in the Gallery
of Battles of the château of Versailles, where it remains.

198

[Philippe-Joseph-Auguste Vallot (1796–1840)]
after Antoine-Jean, Baron Gros (1771–1835)
Napoleon visiting the battlefield of Eylau

198 (b)

Account of the persons in the previous engraving
Musée national des châteaux de Malmaison et Bois-Préau; MM 58–3–60;
Gift of Princess George of Greece, 1958 (formerly the Demidoff Collection,
Prince of San Donato, later to Prince Roland Bonaparte, the donor's father)
Black and white engraving on paper
H. 71; L. 89.5
1833

The battle of Eylau, fought on February 7-8, 1807 between the Prussian
and Russian armies on one side and the French on the other, was totally
useless. After this appalling butchery with enormous losses (20,000 men
on each side) Napoleon had not destroyed the Russian army nor had his
adversaries succeeded in freeing the besieged strongpoints on the
Vistula. Three months later the campaign began again on the same
terrain. Napoleon's propaganda machine touted Eylau as a victory, to be
celebrated by a competition opened in 1807. Gros painted the Emperor
visiting the battlefield after the fighting was done, on February 9, 1807.
Stunned by the carnage, he stayed there for eight days to bring aid
to the wounded, the only time he did so. Gros's masterpiece is now
in the Louvre museum.

199

Louis-Philibert Debucourt (1755–1832), after Horace Vernet (1789–1863)
The Battle of Somo Sierra
Musée national des châteaux de Malmaison et Bois-Préau; MM 58-3-54 bis;
Gift of Princess George of Greece, 1958 (formerly the Demidoff Collection,
Prince of San Donato, later to Prince Roland Bonaparte, the donor's father)
Black and white engraving
H. 64.5; L. 88
1817

More a skirmish than a battle proper, Somo Sierra was named after a narrow pass that
constituted the only obstacle closing the road to Madrid. As the French forces were having
trouble getting through the gorge, on November 30, 1808 Napoleon sent in the unblooded
3rd squadron of Polish lancers whose dogged fighting routed the Spanish defenders; the
way to Madrid lay open. The painting, for which Horace Vernet was paid 2,400 francs in
1816, was translated into an engraving the following year by Debucourt.

200

Jean-Pierre-Marie Jazet (1788-1871), after Hippolyte Bellangé (1800-1866)

The Batlle of Essling

Musée national des châteaux de Malmaison et Bois-Préau; MM 58–3–50 bis;
Gift of Princess George of Greece, 1958 (formerly the Davidoff Collection,
Prince of San Donato, later to Prince Roland Bonaparte, the donor's father)
Black and white engraving
H. 73; L. 102
About 1830

While Napoleon was occupied in reinforcing his brother Joseph's position as King of Spain,
he soon had to face a new coalition beginning to confront him in Germany and Austria.
This was for him the start of difficult and even disputed victories such as the battle of
Essling, which took place May 21- 22, 1809. Losses were considerable on both sides, and
although the village of Essling remained in French hands the Emperor lost one of his most
faithful companions, Marshal Lannes. The print is a reproduction of the great painting
by Bellangé, commissioned in 1836 by Louis-Philippe for the château of Versailles, where
it remains.

201

Jean-Pierre-Marie Jazet (1788–1871) after Horace Vernet (1789–1863)

The Battle of Wagram

Musée national des châteaux de Malmaison et Bois-Préau; unnumbered;
Gift of Princess George of Greece, 1958 (formerly the Davidoff Collection,
Prince of San Donato, later to Prince Roland Bonaparte, the donor's father)
Black and white engraving
H. 57; L. 66
About 1830

The Emperor needed to move nearer to Vienna, but to do so he had to cross the Danube.
The first attempt, at Essling, failed but the second at Wagram on July 5-6 1809 was
successful. The victory was hard won, however, and the French army had trouble pursuing
the Austrians; the Archduke Charles escaped. For the second time Napoleon made his base
at Schönbrunn and dictated his conditions for peace: the Illyrian provinces to be ceded
to France, the payment of a heavy indemnity of war and the ceding of further territories to
the Emperor's allies (which for the Emperor of Austria meant the loss of four million of
his subjects). An indirect consequence of the truce was the "delivery" by Austria of the
Archduchess Marie-Louise when Napoleon was considering marrying again. It is
interesting that near the end of her life Marie-Louise went by train to Wagram to visit
the site of the battle that had changed her life. The painting was commissioned from
Horace Vernet in 1835 for the Gallery of Battles at Versailles, where it remains.

202

Jean-Pierre-Marie Jazet (1788–1871), after Louis-Eugène Lami (1800–1890)

Napoleon at Montereau

Musée national des châteaux de Malmaison et Bois-Préau; MM 58–3–61;
Gift of Princess George of Greece, 1958 (formerly the Davidoff Collection, Prince of San Donato, later to Prince Roland Bonaparte, the donor's father)
Black and white engraving
H. 64.5; L. 73.6
1830

French defeats in Germany in 1813 brought about many defections: almost the whole of Europe decided to have done with Napoleon. It was now a question of defending France herself, no longer of planning new conquests. Moving with amazing speed, Napoleon tried to fool the enemy about the strength of his manpower. There began the incredible campaign of France; after the victories of Champaubert and Montmirail, on February 18, 1814 at Montereau Napoleon repulsed the army of Silesia which nevertheless managed to retreat in disorder without being crushed as Napoleon had hoped. It was at Montereau that, as he was laying the artillery pieces alongside his soldiers, who were worried at seeing him expose himself to enemy fire, the Emperor told them: "The cannon ball that can kill me has yet to be made". This remark was to be spread abroad as part of the Napoleonic legend, starting in the 1830s.

205

Jean-Pierre-Marie Jazet (1788–1871), after Horace Vernet (1789–1863); "firm of Goupil and Vibert"

The Fontainebleau Farewells

Musée national des châteaux de Malmaison et Bois-Préau;
unnumbered;
Gift of Princess George of Greece, 1958 (formerly the Davidoff Collection, Prince of San Donato, later to Prince Roland Bonaparte, the donor's father)
Black and white engraving
H. 85; L. 1.18
1829

Defeated in battle and unable to rally Paris, which was already occupied by the Allies, Napoleon sought refuge in the palace of Fontainebleau, arriving there the evening of March 31, 1814. Although his troops were in good heart, pressure from his Marshals, who were weary of fighting, induced him to sign his first abdication in favour of his son on April 4, and an unconditional abdication on April 6. After trying to poison himself in the night of April 13 to 14 he made up his mind to accept the sovereignty of the island of Elba and left Fontainebleau on April 20. It was just before his departure, in the courtyard of the Cheval Blanc, that Napoleon made his famous speech of farewell to the soldiers of the Old Guard and kissed the flag presented to him by General Petit. The painting was commissioned from Horace Vernet in 1825 by Colonel Auguste Pelletier de Chambure, a passionate supporter of the Emperor, who in 1824 published " Napoleon and His Contemporaries".

216 (b)

Account of the persons in the following print

Musée national des châteaux de Malmaison et Bois-Préau;
unnumbered
Gift of Princess George of Greece, 1958 (formerly the Davidoff Collection, Prince of San Donato, later to Prince Roland Bonaparte, the donor's father)
Black and white engraving
H. 87; L. 1.07
1827

The Treaty of Fontainebleau (April 11, 1814) designated the island of Elba, French since 1802, as Napoleon's new home. He was to keep the title of Emperor, receive an annual revenue of two million francs and exercise sovereignty over the island. Napoleon landed in his capital, Portoferraio, on May 3, 1814 and in ten months completely reorganised Elba, leaving his definitive mark on it. But news of French discontent under Bourbon rule had reached the Emperor. Although heavily guarded for fear he should be kidnapped, he seized on the non-payment of his dues from the French government as a reason for returning and managed to leave the island, evading the enemy fleet. On March 1, 1815 he landed at Golfe-Juan. On his way across the Alps to Grenoble he found the road blocked by a battalion of the 5th regiment of line infantry. Walking forward alone towards the soldiers, he addressed them: "Soldiers of the Fifth, you know me! If there is any one among you who wants to kill his General, his Emperor, he can: here I am". In high emotion the infantrymen acclaimed their Emperor, and on March 20 he reached the Tuileries, borne along by a deliriously joyful crowd.

216

Jean-Pierre-Marie Jazet (1788–1871), after Karl-August von Steuben (1788–1856)

The Return from Elba

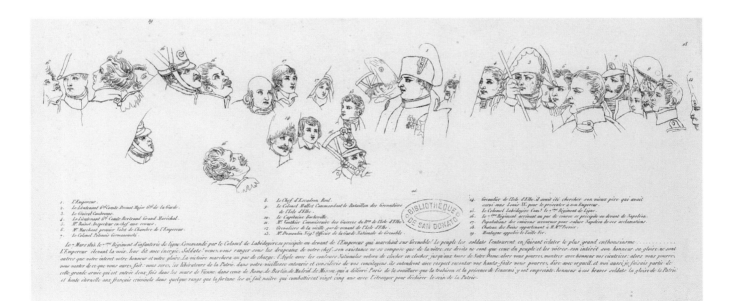

206

Jean-Pierre-Marie Jazet (1788–1871),
after Karl-August von Steuben (1788–1856)

The Battle of Waterloo

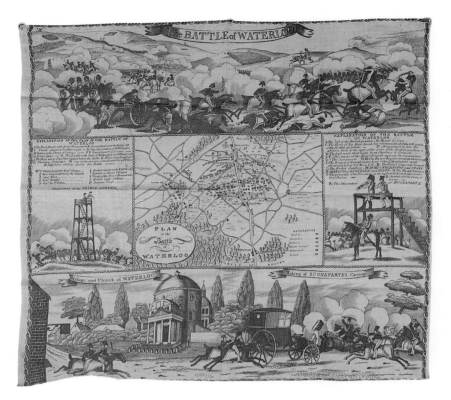

207

Slack

The Battle of Waterloo

Musée national des châteaux
de Malmaison et Bois-Préau (Fonds Napoléon);
N 465; Purchase, 1979 (formerly the collection
of the Imperial family)
Copperplate engraving on cotton
H. 55; L. 59.5
About 1815

206 (b)

Account of the persons in the preceding print

Musée national des châteaux
de Malmaison et Bois-Préau;
MM 40–47–9697; Gift of Lauta
Black and white engraving
H. 86.5; L. 1.17
1836

Napoleon's return to power was bound to rekindle the
conflict: the Allies wanted rid of "the Corsican ogre".
In the hope of forestalling another invasion of France,
Napoleon decided to lead his army in person and attack
the enemy forces at the gates of Brussels where they
were still encamped. The campaign of 1815 was to be
his last. Although the Prussians were beaten on June 16
at Ligny, where they lost 15,000 men, the rest of their
forces managed to withdraw and re-form to march to
support the English two days later. Napoleon, thinking
himself free of the Prussians, decided to attack
Wellington's English army, confronting them on
June 18 at Waterloo.

The battle that would decide Napoleon's fate
took place on June 18 at Waterloo. Misled about
the position of the Prussians, whom he thought
far from the scene of operations, Napoleon still
hoped to beat the English; but instead of
Grouchy's reinforcements it was Blücher's army
that appeared, and their arrival settled the
outcome of the battle. From then on it was all
over, and despite many acts of heroism the French
had to sound the retreat. The Emperor hastily
returned to Paris and the Élysée palace, abdicating
on June 22. This scarf or neckerchief, of English
manufacture, shows the order of battle framed
by the observation posts of the Prince of Orange
and of Napoleon; the upper part shows the battle
itself, the lower the pillaging of the Emperor's
carriage. Shortly afterwards this kind of scarf was
being sold to tourists on the battlefield itself.

209

Coat of an officer of the militia of Lower Canada

Montreal, The Stewart Museum at the Fort, Île Sainte-Hélène;
inv. 1978.3.2 (from Musée du Château Ramezay)
Red and green woollen cloth, brass buttons
H. 78
Canada; about 1810

This coat may have belonged to Colonel Salaberry.
Charles-Michel de Salaberry (1778-1829) was a lieutenant in
the 60th Regiment of Foot by 1794. He served in the West Indies
(Guadeloupe, Martinique, Jamaica), in Ireland in 1808 and in
Holland in 1809 as a brigadier. Returning to Canada in 1810 he
served in the Royal American Regiment with the same rank.
In 1811-1812 he raised a corps of light infantry for the militia of
Lower Canada called *les Voltigeurs* (the Riflemen). Promoted
to lieutenant-colonel, he led these men against the Americans
on October 26, 1813 in the dramatic battle of Châteauguay,
earning the name of "the Hero of Châteauguay". He later
became a prosperous landowner by 1814, a justice of the
peace in 1815 and a member of the Legislative Council in 1818.
Salaberry was opposed to the union of the two Canadas in 1822.
He died in his home at Chambly in 1829.
G.V.

204

Uniform of a British soldier of the 83rd Regiment of Foot

Salon-de-Provence, Château-Musée de l'Empéri
(formerly the Raoul and Jean Brunon Collection)

In 1794 the 83rd Regiment of Foot was
incorporated under this name, which it kept
until 1859. The regiment fought in Spain from
1809 to 1814, distinguishing itself at Talavera
(1809), Busaco (1810), Fuentes de Oñoro (1811),
Ciudad Rodrigo (1813), Badajoz and Salamanca
(1812), Vitoria, Nivelle and Orthes (1813). The
regiment finally occupied Toulouse in 1814 after
the English army crossed the Pyrenees. Line
infantry was at the forefront of every battle
and constituted the backbone of every nation's
army. The lot of the foot soldiers of the time in
any army was not a happy one: they had only
their two legs to carry them across Europe and
their two arms to fight with, more often than
not on an empty stomach with a parched
mouth, at the mercy of their officers' marching
orders.
G.V.

208
Coat of an officer in the militia of Lower Canada

Montreal, The Stewart Museum at the Fort,
Île Sainte-Hélène; inv. 1978.3.1
(from Musée du château Ramezay)
Red and green woollen cloth, brass buttons
H. 78 cm
Canada; about 1810

The militias formed in English colonies adopted
uniforms similar to English ones – the scarlet coat,
the shako, the weapons. However, militia officers could
wear only one epaulette in addition to the gorget with
the royal coat-of-arms. The militia in Canada goes back
to the days of the French colony where Governor
Frontenac organised the first corps of militia (1670).
Seeing how efficient this system was, the English
coopted those same officers of militia as soon as
the conquest was achieved, which explains why most
militia officers in Lower Canada thereafter were of
French-Canadian origin.
G.V.

210
English cavalry officer's sabre, 1796 model

Montreal, The Stewart Museum at the Fort,
Île Sainte-Hélène; inv. 1974.23.76
Steel, shagreen
L. 92.5
Great Britain; about 1800

This cavalry officer's sword is identical to the model
produced that year for troopers. The blued-steel blade,
engraved or gilded, marked it out as an officer's
weapon.
G.V.

211
English musician's sword

Montreal, The Stewart Museum at the Fort,
Île Sainte-Hélène; inv. 1974.23.87
Steel, brass
L. 86.2
Great Britain; about 1800

After 1800 a certain uniformity can be seen in the
swords of English military musicians. The influence
of the Egyptian campaign (1797-1801) is apparent in the
shape and the Mameluke-style hilt of the musicians'
weapon. Hilts adorned with lion, tiger, eagle and horse
heads were common, as was the curved blade.
G.V.

212
**English infantry officer's
sword, 1796 model**

Montreal, The Stewart Museum
at the Fort, Île Sainte-Hélène;
inv. 1973.23.40
Steel, brass, silver
L. 79.5
Great Britain; about 1800

The 1796 type of officer's
sword continued in use for
over a quarter century. Note
that one of the flanges of
the hilt is hinged for comfort.
G.V.

213

Edward Walsh, draughtsman (1756–1832)
and John Black, engraver

**A view of the City of Montreal and the River St. Lawrence from the Mountain, London.
Published Jan. 1, 1811, at R. Ackermann's Repository of Arts, 101 Strand.**

Montreal, The Stewart Museum at the Fort, Île Sainte-Hélène; inv. 1970.960.2
Colour engraving
H. 42.7; L.56.1
London, England; 1811

214

Lemaître direxit

The Nelson Monument, Montreal

Montreal, The Stewart Museum at the Fort, Île Sainte-Hélène;
inv. 1970.1027
Copperplate engraving
H. 15.5; L. 11
Paris, France; 1829

Of all the colonies in the British Empire it was in Lower Canada, in Montreal, that the very first monument was erected to the glory of Admiral Nelson and the victory of Trafalgar (October 21, 1805). It was commissioned by the merchants of the city and the project entrusted to the London architect Mitchell. The corner-stone of the monument was laid on August 17, 1809. There was still, however, a segment of the population of Lower Canada hoping to be reunited with France. The fear of insurrection was real: on August 13, 1803 notice of expulsion was served on all subjects of the French Republic who had come to Canada since 1792. In 1805 Milnes, Secretary of State for the Colonies, reassured the colonial authorities about the supposedly belligerent intentions of the French and cancelled the notice of expulsion. On March 1, 1805 a dozen inhabitants of Saint-Constant, a village south of Montreal, addressed a petition to the Emperor Napoleon asking him to do something so that the French-Canadian people might again bear "the glorious name of Frenchmen". No concrete proposal to this effect was ever made by the Imperial government.
G.V.

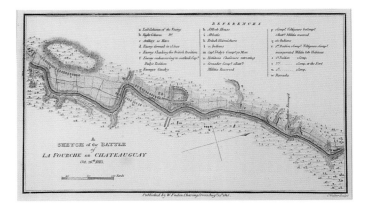

215

J. Walker

A Sketch of the Battle of La Fourche or Châteauguay Oct 26ᵗʰ 1813, Published by W. Faden, Charing Cross Aug'st 12ᵗʰ 1815. J. Walker Sculpt.

Montreal, The Stewart Museum at the Fort, Île Sainte-Hélène;
inv. 1982.382
Coloured copperplate engraving
H. 13.8; L. 23
London, England; 1815

The main reasons why the United States of America declared war on England on June 19, 1812 were the enforced enrolment of American sailors aboard vessels of the Royal Navy, the harassing of American merchant ships by the English along the American coast, the violation of American neutrality and the English refusal to lift the blockade of European ports. The initial American offensives targeted Upper Canada: the Niagara peninsula. Detroit and Niagara were used as bases for the American troops, who in 1813, captured Toronto (then called York) and burned it down. An attack on Montreal was attempted that same year but was stopped at Chrysler's Farm (Brockville, Ontario) on the St. Lawrence river and on the banks of the Chateauguay at La Fourche, near Ormstown, Quebec. Lieutenant-colonel Charles-Michel de Salaberry, at the head of 300 Voltigeurs and over a hundred militiamen and Mohawks in ambush behind some brushwood, routed the vanguard of an American army of more than 7,000 men under the command of General Hampton. This single first attack was enough to turn back the Americans, who had been marching to Montreal. The Treaty of Ghent, signed in 1814, put an end to hostilities.
G.V.

VI

1815-1821

VI

Napoleon on St. Helena

217

Jean-Baptiste-Claude-<u>Eugène</u> Guillaume
(1822–1905)

Napoleon in 1820

Musée national des châteaux
de Malmaison et Bois-Préau;
MM 40–47–6847;
Gift of Madame Henri Lefuel,
descendent of the sculptor
Plaster
H. 70; L. 60
Second Empire

This bust is one of a series of six
sculpted portraits of Napoleon at
different stages of his life.

Abandoned by everyone, Napoleon stopped for a few days at Malmaison and then travelled
to the Ile d'Aix near La Rochelle, possibly with an idea of retreating
to the United States; it was on this small island that he took the decision to
surrender to the English (July 1815), hoping to end his days respected in the midst
of his enemies. But after taking him to Plymouth the English informed him that
he was to be transported to St. Helena, a tiny volcanic islet lost in the middle
of the south Atlantic, suggested as the place of detention by Wellington himself.
After a voyage of almost two and a half months, Napoleon with a handful of faithful
followers landed on St. Helena, the last stage of his "Epic", on October 16, 1815.

The island, about the size of Paris and over 2,500 kilometres from the nearest land, offered the English the best possible guarantee of security. There Napoleon was to spend almost six years, cut off from the world in a modest house called Longwood and surrounded by enemies who recognised him only as General Bonaparte. To show the English that he was still and always the Emperor Napoleon, he instituted strict ceremony and etiquette as if he were still at the Tuileries. The strict application of his orders by Governor Hudson Lowe poisoned daily life, restricting the freedom of the French exiles.

Napoleon divided his time almost equally between work and relaxation, the latter in the form of endless conversations which his followers hastened to transcribe as memoirs to be published on their return to Europe. Living at such close quarters inevitably brought about misunderstandings among the Emperor's companions in misfortune, which were aggravated by the jealousy of Madame Bertrand and Madame de Montholon. Some went back to Europe, and Longwood gradually emptied just as the Emperor's health was beginning to give cause for concern. The ministrations of the newly arrived Dr. Antommarchi were of no help. On January 1, 1821 the Emperor told his friends that he would not see the year out. Knowing that he was sinking, he summoned up what little strength he had left to dictate his last wishes to General Montholon and thus to reward the last of the faithful. On May 5, 1821 at 5.49 p.m. the man who had made the world tremble for over twenty years breathed his last, as a result, according to the latest medical hypotheses, of the perforation of a benign gastric ulcer in the left lobe of an already diseased liver. Other theories postulate different causes, from stomach cancer to poisoning; the question will always arouse debate.

On May 9 Napoleon was buried in Geranium Valley – thereafter to be called Tomb Valley – in the presence of English troops who paid him the honours due to an ordinary general in the British Army. The remains were to stay there for almost twenty years before France could bring them home for proper burial. It was not until October 15, 1840 that French soldiers under the command of the Prince de Joinville, son of King Louis-Philippe, landed on St. Helena from the ship and exhumed the Emperor's body to take it back to Paris. On December 15 of the same year the heavy coffin was borne down the Champs-Élysées, watched by huge crowds, to the Invalides, where Napoleon rests according to his wishes "on the banks of the Seine in the midst of the French people he had so greatly loved."

219

Franz Gerasch (1826- ?)
and Johann-Joseph Rauch (about 1803- ?),
after Horace Vernet (1789–1863)

Napoleon on St. Helena
Musée national des châteaux
de Malmaison et Bois-Préau;
MM 40–47–7237; Gift of M. Émile Brouwet
Colour lithograph, published in Vienna
H. 48; L. 38
About 1825

This unusual portrait of Napoleon corresponds
to reality; the Musée de Malmaison has most
of the clothes illustrated in the print. We know
that towards the end of his life Napoleon wanted
to take some exercise and in 1819 tried his hand
at gardening, an activity he soon gave up.

218

Louis-Joseph-Narcisse, Comte Marchand (1791–1876)

View of Longwood, St. Helena

Boulogne-Billancourt, bibliothèque Marmottan; inv. 70–151
Watercolour, gouache
H. 33; L. 47
1821

On October 17, 1815 Napoleon and his companions in exile landed on St. Helena, a tiny
island lost in the middle of the Atlantic Ocean 2,500 kilometres from the coast of Africa.
After lodging for two months at The Briars with the Balcombes, Napoleon moved into
Longwood House on December 10. He was to spend five and a half years in this house,
which was nothing but the summer residence of a lieutenant-governor enamoured of
solitude. It turned out far too small to hold the Emperor and his entourage, so the British
enlarged it. Longwood was purchased by Napoleon III in 1858, and since then has been
listed as state property administered by the French Ministry of Foreign Affairs through
extraterritorial prerogatives.

220

The Emperor's dressing gown
Musée national des châteaux
de Malmaison et Bois-Préau (Fonds Napoléon);
N 266; Gift of T.I.H. Prince and Princess
Napoleon Bonaparte, 1979
Cotton piqué
H. 130
Early-19th century

First purveyed by the tailor Chevalier and
then by his successor Lejeune, these white
cotton dressing-gowns could also be worn
as frockcoats. The Emperor wore them a great
deal; on St. Helena he put one on in the
morning and did not usually take it off before
his early-afternoon bath. Of the eight robes
taken into exile, two went to Marshal
Bertrand after the Emperor's death and were
bequeathed by his daughter Hortense Thayer
to Prince Victor Napoleon (both in the Musée
de Malmaison).

221

The Emperor's underwear
Musée national des châteaux
de Malmaison et Bois-Préau (Fonds Napoléon);
N 282; Gift of T.I.H. Prince and Princesse
Napoleon Bonaparte, 1979
Cotton
L. 110
Early-19th century

This underwear was made of very fine linen
or fustian. On top, Napoleon wore white
cashmere breeches held at the knee with
a small gold buckle.

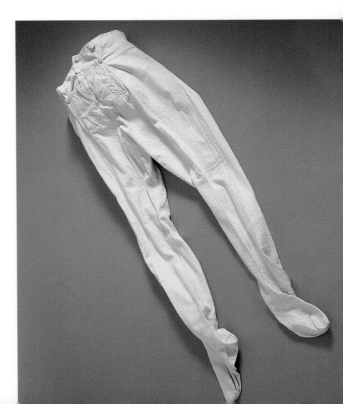

225

Shirt of the Emperor

Musée national des châteaux de Malmaison
et Bois-Préau (Fonds Napoléon);
N 304; Gift of T.I.H. Prince Napoleon
Bonaparte and Countess de Witt, 1979
Flannel
H. 70; L. 35
Early-19th century

On St. Helena the Emperor had 87 cambric shirts left; each had required 2.88 metres of cambric for the making. The shirts came, under the Empire, from Mesdemoiselles Lolive and de Beuvry, linen-drapers to Their Imperial and Royal Majesties, at 48 francs apiece. Napoleon always wore beautiful clothes, most embroidered with his monogram, a crowned N, and they cost a great deal. He was allowed to take much of his wardrobe to St. Helena. The Emperor bequeathed six shirts to his son and each executor of the will received twenty-seven of them.

227

Stockings of the Emperor

Toronto, The Bata Shoe Museum;
inv. P 96.0075 A-D
Black silk
L. 35.2; W. 24.5
Early-19th century

After putting his shirt on, the valet placed on the Emperor's feet very light merino-wool undersocks over which he pulled white or somethimes black silk stockings held up by elastic suspenders. The Emperor's stockings usually came from Panier and cost 18 francs apiece, which caused him to say: "Why more expensive for me than for anyone else? I don't understand it. Ought I to be robbed?". This pair, worn by Napoleon on St. Helena, were given by Madame Bertrand, wife of the Emperor's great Marshal, to Dr. Dickson, surgeon of the English ship *Camel* which brought the Bertrands back to Europe after Napoleon's death.

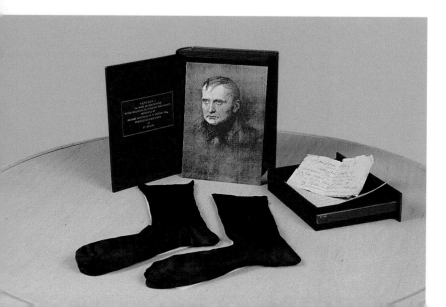

223

Straw hat belonging to the Emperor
Musée national des châteaux de Malmaison
et Bois-Préau (Fonds Napoléon);
N 292; Gift of T.I.H. Prince Napoleon Bonaparte
and Countess de Witt, 1979
Straw, silk
H. 17; D. 42
Early-19th century

This hat, the only such in the Emperor's
wardrobe, he wore to protect against the
sun when he went out into his garden at
Longwood. It appears in an inventory of
Napoleon's effects drawn up after his death
by Marchand. It is a wide-brimmed Panama
hat with a white silk lining inside which was
found a cutting from an English newspaper,
which suggests that the hat was locally
made. Courtesy of Madame Thayer.

222

**Madras scarf worn by the Emperor
on St. Helena**
Musée national des châteaux de Malmaison
et Bois-Préau (Fonds Napoléon);
N 314; Gift of T.I.H.. Prince Napoleon Bonaparte
and Countess de Witt, 1979
Cotton
L. 75; W. 75
Early-19th century

When he got up during the night to work
Napoleon used to tie a red-and-white
checked cotton scarf or madras round his
head. Of the 19 scarves found after his death
three are in the Musée de Malmaison; this
one was given to Prince Victor Napoléon by
Madame Thayer, Marshal Bertrand's
daughter.

224

Slippers of the Emperor
Musée national des châteaux de Malmaison
et Bois-Préau (Fonds Napoléon);
N 297; Gift of T.I.H. Prince Napoleon Bonaparte
and Countess de Witt, 1979
Leather
L. 26
Early-19th century

The Emperor wore these red leather slippers
continually on St. Helena; they are found in
the after-death inventory of his effects, and
then were the property of Madame Thayer.

226

Francesco Antommarchi (1789–1838),
the Emperor's doctor on St. Helena

Napoleon's death mask, Antommarchi's own copy

Musée national des châteaux de Malmaison et Bois-Préau;
MM 40–47–7284; Purchase, 1944
Plaster
H. 35; L. 15
About 1821

To make the Emperor's death mask the Irish doctor Francis Burton
(1787-1828) had the idea of grinding up the gypsum he had collected
on the island beaches; he may have mixed this with ground-up plaster
statuettes he had bought in Jamestown. It appears that the Corsican
physician Francesco Antommarchi (1789-1838) may have spirited away
the facial part of the mask with the help of Madame Bertrand, wife of
the great marshal. Trying to restore the missing bits they made several
copies from the original mask shown here, the doctor's own. In 1833
Antommarchi organised a subscription fund whereby anyone could
acquire the Emperor's death mask. Made of plaster or bronze, each
mask bore Antommarchi's signature on the side and in front a small
bronze medallion with the Emperor's laurelled head in profile. King
Louis-Philippe subscribed for five copies in bronze and twenty-five in
plaster.

228

Eagle

Musée national des châteaux
de Malmaison et Bois-Préau
(Fonds Napoléon); unnumbered;
Gift of T.I.H. Prince and Princess
Napoléon Bonaparte, 1981
Gilded wood
H. 85; L. 160
First or Second Empire

Many gilt-wood eagles are still extant;
they were made for official celebrations
of the régime in both the First and the
Second Empire.

Charles-Marie Bonaparte
(1746–85)
m. 1764

Maria Letizia Ramolino
(1750–1836)

Joseph
(1768–1844)
King of Naples
1806–8
then King of Spain
1808–13

m. 1794
Julie Clary
(1771–1845)

Napoleon I
(1769–1821)
Emperor of the French
1804–14 and 1815

m. 1796
1) Marie-Joseph-Rose
de Tascher de la Pagerie
called Josephine
(1763–1814)
divorced in 1809

m. 1810
2) Marie-Louise
Archduchess of Austria
(1791–1847)

Napoleon II
(1811–32)
King of Rome
Duke of Reichstadt
(unmarried)

Lucien
(1775–1840)
first Prince of
Canino, 1814

m. 1794
1) Christine Boyer
(1773–1800)

m. 1803
2) Alexandrine Jacob
de Bleschamp
(1778–1855)

Élisa
(Maria-Anna)
(1777–1820)
Grand Duchess
of Toscany
1809–14

m. 1797
Félix Bacciochi
Prince of
Massa-Carrara
(1762–1841)

Louis
(1778–1846)
King of Holland
1806–10

m. 1802
Hortense
de Beauharnais
(1783–1837)

Pauline
(Maria-Paoletta)
(1780–1825)
Duchess of Guastalla
1806–14

m. 1797
Victor-Emmanuel Leclerc
(1772–1802)

m. 1803
Camille
Prince Borghèse
(1775–1832)

Caroline
(Maria-Anunziata)
(1782–1839)
Grand Duchess of Berg
1806–8

m. 1800
Joachim Murat
(1767–1815)
King of Naples
1808–15

Jérôme
(1784–1860)
King of Westphallia
1807–13

m. 1803
Élisabeth Patterson
(1785–1879)
separated in 1806
divorced in 1811

m. 1807
Catherine de Wurtemberg
(1783–1835)

Louis-Napoleon
Napoléon III
(1808–73)
Emperor of the French
(1852–70)

Napoleon
called Prince Napoleon
Jérôme
(1822–91)

m. 1859
Clotilde de Savoie
(1843–1911)

Victor Prince Napoleon
Head of the Imperial House
(1862–1926)

m. 1910
Clémentine of Belgium
(1872–1955)

Louis Prince Napoleon
Head of the Imperial House
(1914–97)

m. 1949
Alix de Foresta
(born 1926)
two sons and two daughters

The name Malmaison (bad dwelling) probably came from the establishment of a ninth-century Viking camp on the site of the present castle, from which the Norsemen made sorties to pillage and burn neighbouring villages. As a fiefdom of the powerful Abbey of Saint-Denis, like the village of Rueil, Malmaison first appears in 1244 as a simple farm. In the fourteenth century the first fortified manor-house was built; the land remained in the same family from 1390 to 1763. In about 1610-1620 Christophe Perrot, Councillor to the Parliament of Paris, had the old manor rebuilt in the style then fashionable, with high slate roofs and pavilions crowned with semi-circular pediments. The building was initially enlarged in 1686-1687, and the two wings looking on to the courtyard were added in about 1780.

In 1771 the chateau was purchased by a wealthy financier, Jacques-Jean Le Couteulx du Molay, who with his wife entertained select guests including the painter Madame Vigée Lebrun and the poet Marmontel. The Le Couteulx were beggared by the Revolution and obliged to sell their home. On April 21, 1799 it came into the hands of Josephine Bonaparte, wife to the famous general then still in Egypt. Between 1800 and 1802 Malmaison became, together with the Tuileries, the seat of government; there ministers foregathered to reorganise a France bled white by the Revolution. Two young architects, Percier and Fontaine, redecorated the rooms in the antique style then so fashionable. This was the chateau's most brilliant period: Bonaparte came here to relax at weekends, playing blind-man's-buff and enjoying concerts, balls and entertainments in the little theatre, now gone.

Josephine, crowned empress on December 2, 1804, continued to improve the estate, although Napoleon's visits became rare. She had Thibault and Vignon design a hothouse, enabling her to acclimatise the rarest plant species painted by Redouté; Berthault her architect built for her a grand gallery, since demolished, which she filled with works of art, paintings, Greek vases and statues. After the divorce, in December 1809, Josephine retired to Malmaison, where Berthault refitted the drawing-room, the billiard room and the bedroom in which she died on May 29, 1814 as the result of a neglected sore throat.

She bequeathed the chateau to her son Prince Eugène (died 1824), whose widow sold it to the Swedish banker Jonas Hagerman; it was then stripped of all its furnishings. Queen Cristina, the exiled queen of Spain, purchased Malmaison in 1842. In 1861 she sold it to Napoleon III, Josephine's grandson, who first opened it as a museum for the Universal Exhibition of 1867. In 1870 the property was damaged in the fighting of the Franco-Prussian War (1870-1871), and in 1877 it was sold by the French government to a developer who set about dividing up the estate. The chateau together with a six-hectare (fifteen-acre) plot was purchased in 1896 by the philanthropist Daniel Iffla, nicknamed Osiris, who gave it to the nation in 1904. The Malmaison Museum opened in 1906.

1769 August 15
Napoleon Bonaparte born in Ajaccio.

1779 May 15
Enters Military College of Brienne.

1784 October 17
Enters the Royal Military College of Paris.
Graduates out October 28, 1785 with
the rank of Second Lieutenant, and is
stationed at Valence in the Rhone Valley.

1786 September-
1793 June
Stationed at Auxonne, Burgundy; visits
Corsica five times.

1793 December
Siege of Toulon where he is noticed and
promoted to Brigadier General.

1795 October 5
Helps to crush the royalist uprising
at the request of Director Barras; first
meets Josephine; promoted to General-
in-command, Army of the Interior.

1796 March 9
Marries Josephine in a civil ceremony.

1796 March-
1797 October
First Italian campaign. Defeats
Austrians at Lodi, Arcola and Rivoli.
Treaty of Campo-Formio.

1798 May-
1799 October
Egyptian campaign, ending in
Bonaparte's hasty return to Paris.

1799 November 9-10
Coup of 18 Brumaire by which he seizes
power. Elected First Consul of the
Republic, he declares the Revolution at
an end.

1800 May-June
Second Italian campaign,
Austrians defeated at Marengo.

1802 March 25
Peace of Amiens signed with England.

1802 August 4
Bonaparte appointed Consul for life.

1803 May 16
Peace of Amiens breaks down.

1804 May 18
Bonaparte proclaimed Emperor
of the French.

1804 December 2
Crowned by Pope Pius VII.

1805 March 17
Crowned King of Italy in Milan.

1805 April-December
Third coalition of England, Naples,
Russia and Austria against France;
destruction of the French fleet at
Trafalgar; the coalition dissolves after
Napoleon's victory at Austerlitz and
the Peace of Presbourg.

1806 October
Fourth coalition of England, Prussia and
Russia against France; Napoleon gains
victories at Jena and Auerstadt, enters
Berlin.

1807 June 14
The Russians are defeated at Friedland;
peace Treaty of Tilsit signed by Czar
Alexander and Napoleon.

1808 February 20
Start of the occupation of Spain, which
never completely surrenders; Napoleon
has to withdraw his troops in April 1813.

1809 April-October
Fifth coalition of England and Austria
against France. The Austrians are
defeated at Wagram; Napoleon enters
Vienna.

1809 December 15
Napoleon divorces Josephine.

1810 April 2
Church marriage of Napoleon and the
Archduchess Marie-Louise of Austria.

1811 March 20
Birth of the King of Rome, son of
Napoleon and Marie-Louise.

1812 June-December
The Russian campaign; for the first
time Napoleon is forced to retreat;
the Grand Army is decimated.

1813 March-November
Sixth coalition of England, Austria,
Prussia and Russia against France;
following the allied victory at the battle
of Leipzig (October 15), Napoleonic
Germany collapses and Holland is lost.

1814 January-March
Allied troops enter France and despite
a brilliant French defence, enter Paris
on March 31.

1814 April 4
Napoleon abdicates unconditionally
at Fontainebleau.

1814 May 4-
1815 February 26
Napoleon is permitted to keep his title
of Emperor and is made ruler of Elba,
an island off the coast of Italy.

1815 March-June
Napoleon escapes from Elba, returns to
Paris and reigns again for three months
(the Hundred Days).

1815 June 18
Wellington and Blücher defeat
Napoleon completely at Waterloo.

1815 June 22
Napoleon's second abdication, from the
Elysée Palace, Paris. He travels to the
Ile d'Aix, where he decides to surrender
to the English (July 15).

1815 October 16
Napoleon lands on St. Helena, where he
remains in exile for five and a half years.

1821 May 5
Napoleon dies at Longwood, St. Helena.

1840 December 15
Return of the Ashes; the Emperor's
remains are entombed in the Invalides.

*"Your sovereigns, born to the throne,
can be defeated twenty times and still
return to their capitals: I cannot, because
I am a jumped-up soldier. My dominion
will not outlive me, from the day I am
no longer strong and therefore no
longer to be feared."*

– Napoleon to Metternich,
Chancellor of Austria.

Selected Bibliography

ARMINJON, Catherine, BLONDEL, Nicole, *Objets civils domestiques, Vocabulaire typologique*, Paris, Imprimerie nationale (Principes d'analyse scientifique), 1984.

ARMINJON, Catherine, BEAUPUIS, James, BILIMOFF, Michèle et Bernard, EMMANUELLI *Dictionnaire des poinçons de fabricants d'ouvrages d'or et d'argent de Paris et de la Seine, 1798-1838*, Paris, Imprimerie Nationale, Inventaire Général des Monuments et des Richesses Artistiques de la France, (Cahiers de l'Inventaire 25), 1991.

BIMBENET-PRIVAT, Michèle, DE FONTAINES, Gabriel, préface par Jean Dérens, *La datation de l'orfèvrerie parisienne sous l'Ancien régime, Poinçons de jurande et poinçons de la Marque 1507-1792*, Paris, Paris-Musées, Éditions des Musées de la Ville de Paris, 1995.

BOURGUIGNON, Jean, *Napoléon Bonaparte*, 2 volumes, Paris, Les Editions Nationales, 1936.

FIERRO, Alfred, PALLUEL-GUILLARD, André et Jean TULARD, *Histoire et dictionnaire du Consulat et de l'Empire*, Paris, Laffont, 1995.

GANIERE, Paul, *Napoléon à Sainte-Hélène*, 3 volumes, Paris, Libairie Académique Perrin, 1957-1962.

GRANDJEAN, Serge, *L'orfèvrerie du XIXᵉ siècle en Europe*, Paris, Presses Universitaires de France, 1962.

HELFT, Jacques, *Le poinçon des provinces françaises*, Paris, F. de Nobele, 1968 et 1985.
        -*Nouveaux poinçons suivis de recherches techniques et historiques sur l'orfèvrerie sous l'Ancien régime*, Nancy, Éditions Berger-Levrault, 1980.

LEMAIRE, Jean, *Le Testament de Napoléon : un étonnant destin 1821-1857*, Paris, Plon, 1975.

MASSON, Frédéric, *Napoléon chez lui*, Paris, E. Dentu, 1894.
        -*Le Sacre et le Couronnement de Napoléon*, Paris, Albin Michel, 1925.

MAZE-SENCIER, Alphonse, *Les fournisseurs de Napoléon 1ᵉʳ et des deux impératrices*, Paris, Henri Laurens, 1893.

NAPOLEON, *Correspondance de Napoléon 1ᵉʳ publiée par ordre de l'empereur Napoléon III*, 29 volumes, Paris, Imprimerie Impériale, 1858-1869.

SAMOYAULT, Jean-Pierre, SAMOYAULT-VERLET, Colombe, *Château de Fontainebleau, Musée Napoléon 1ᵉʳ*, Paris, Editions de la Réunion des musées nationaux, 1986.

TULARD, Jean, *Napoléon*, Paris, Fayard, 1980.
        - *Dictionnaire Napoléon*, Paris, Fayard, 1987.

TULARD, Jean, GARROS, Louis, *Itinéraire de Napoléon au jour le jour 1769-1821*, Paris, Tallandier, 1992.

Exhibition catalogues

- Paris, Grand Palais, *Napoléon*, 1969.

- Paris, Grand Palais, *Cinq années d'enrichissement du Patrimoine national 1975-1980. Donations, dations, acquisitions*, 1980.

Photographic credits